Working with

Angels

Flowing with *God* in the *Supernatural*

STEVEN W. BROOKS

DESTINY IMAGE® PUBLISHERS, INC.
P.O. Box 310, Shippensburg, PA 17257-0310

*"Speaking to the Purposes of God for this
Generation and for the Generations to Come."*

This book and all other Destiny Image, Revival Press, Mercy Place, Fresh Bread, Destiny Image Fiction, and Treasure House books are available at Christian bookstores and distributors worldwide.

For a U.S. bookstore nearest you, call 1-800-722-6774.
For more information on foreign distributors, call 717-532-3040.
Or reach us on the Internet: www.destinyimage.com

ISBN-10: 0-7684-2511-5
ISBN-13: 978-0-7684-2511-6

For Worldwide Distribution, Printed in the U.S.A.
1 2 3 4 5 6 7 8 9 10 11 / 09 08 07

DEDICATION

This book is dedicated to those fervently devoted saints whom God is raising up today—those who, like Enoch of old, desire to cultivate and experience a deep and pleasing relationship with the Lord Jesus. As you lean into Him more, may all your deepest desires in Him come true.

I also dedicate this book to the saints who have gone before us and paved a way into the deeper waters of God's Spirit. In particular, I express my thanks toward Sadhu Sundar Singh (1889-1929), John Wright Follette (1884-1966), and Dr. John G. Lake (1870-1935). These men were not perfect, but all of them walked in great levels of biblical light and understanding and stood at the forefront of the apostolic and prophetic ministries of their time. Each of these men exemplified a highly developed Christ-like character, shaped through an intimate walk with God that continues to serve as sources of inspiration for believer's today.

ACKNOWLEDGMENTS

I acknowledge and express my thanks to my beautiful wife, Kelly, who sacrificed her time and patience so I could write this book. Without her help, it would not have been accomplished.

I am also grateful to my daughter, Abigail, who provided inspiration for me to write portions of this book because of her deep love for horses.

To Dr. Helen Lang, I express my thanks for the work she did editing the manuscript of this book.

To all of my ministry partners, thank you for your faithful support and prayers. Our God is faithful.

TABLE OF CONTENTS

Foreword

by Wade Taylor

I strongly recommend Steven's book which I have found to be both inspiring and insightful.

Working with Angels will provoke you to embark on a quest for the high spiritual path, which leads toward a realistic and attainable walk with our Lord that promises a rich and lasting reward. I acknowledge this book to be honest and straightforward in what is required to truly *work with angels*.

The real life experiences that Steven eloquently relates, combined with solid scriptural backing, provide a vehicle to explore further into the vast and infinite realms of God's Spirit. There is so much more that God desires for us to experience.

Steven spends many hours praying, meditating, and waiting on the Lord. He is one who longs for revelation and illumination regarding the deeper truths of God's Word. Many of his discoveries and mysteries are unveiled within the pages of this book.

The ministry of the angels that Steven writes about is presently being restored to its proper place within the Church. In these end times, each of us should expect to see a much greater increase of angelic activity within our lives. Steven does a masterful job of clarifying just how we can position ourselves to better work with God's angels, by beautifully illustrating the similarities between horses and angels.

This book carries a fresh impartation from the Spirit of God that is readily transferred to the reader. As you read and meditate on the truths within, you will sense an upward pull on your spirit that carries you to new heights in your walk with the Lord.

Allow this book to create within you an insatiable hunger, and an expectancy to see greater manifestations of our Lord's radiant glory and marvelous wonders in your life.

It's time for God's people to *begin working with angels*!

Wade Taylor
Washington, DC
Author, Founder and President Emeritus
of Pinecrest Bible Training Center

Chapter One

WORKING WITH ANGELS

WORKING WITH ANGELS

In these last days that we are living in before the Lord returns, God desires His people to reap a great harvest of souls, and the angels have a large part to play as all of Heaven teams up for this global event. Many Christians have no idea that God actually expects them to work with the angels to fulfill His plan in the earth.

God expected Moses to work together with the angel that was assigned to help him.

See, I am sending an **angel** *ahead of you to guard you along the way and to bring you to the place I have prepared.* **Pay attention to him and listen to what he says.** *Do not rebel against him; he will not forgive your rebellion, since my Name is in him. If you listen carefully to what he says and do all that I say, I will be an enemy to*

your enemies and oppose those who oppose you. My angel will go ahead of you and bring you into the land of the Amorites, Hittites, Perizzites, Canaanites, Hivites, and Jebusites, and I will wipe them out (Exodus 23:20-23 NIV).

In this case, the Lord guided the people through the angel and placed His name in the angel. The Lord revealed Himself in and through the angel, which is why Jehovah demanded unconditional obedience to the angel's words of instruction. Working with angels is also evident in the life of the prophet Elijah.

> *But **the angel of the LORD said to Elijah** the Tishbite, "Go up and meet the messengers of the king of Samaria and ask them, 'Is it because there is no God in Israel that you are going off to consult Baal-Zebub, the god of Ekron?'"* (2 Kings 1:3 NIV).

King Ahaziah of Israel sent 50 soldiers in three separate divisions to capture Elijah. The first two units and their captains were consumed by fire from Heaven as they stood before Elijah in their pride and arrogance. The third unit of soldiers was spared because their captain recognized an alarming cyclical pattern that was taking place. He humbled himself and pleaded for his life and the life of the 50 men with him. Once the captain's intentions were pure and there was a renewed reverence for the God of Israel, the angel of the Lord spoke again to Elijah.

> **The angel of the LORD said to Elijah, "Go down with him; do not be afraid of him."** *So Elijah got up and went down with him to the king* (2 Kings 1:15 NIV).

Sometimes those who are not educated about the ministry of angels try to explain away such verses by saying,

"That's only for those living in the Old Testament. It only applies to the Jews." Yet, the Book of Acts is in the New Testament, and the apostle Paul had a great working relationship with his ministry angel who saved the lives of over 200 men.

> *After the men had gone a long time without food, Paul stood up before them and said, "Men, you should have taken my advice not to sail from Crete, then you would have spared yourselves this damage and loss. But I urge you to keep up your courage, because not one of you will be lost, only the ship will be destroyed.* **Last night an angel of the God whose I am and whom I serve stood beside me and said, "Do not be afraid, Paul. You must stand trial before Caesar, and God has graciously given you the lives of all who sail with you.** *So keep up your courage, men, for I have faith in God that it will happen just as he told me* (Acts 27:21-25 NIV).

Notice that Paul said an angel stood by him and gave him a message that brought great comfort. Paul had faith in the angel's words because he knew the angel was sent from God. God is still sending angels today to bring vital information of peace and deliverance to the hearer. The reason we do not see more of this kind of activity taking place is because many of God's people are not open to receive this type of ministry.

SEEING ANGELS

I'll never forget my first experience with someone who valued the ministry of the angels.

The year was 1992, and I was sitting in the third row of a large church in Lubbock, Texas. It was a beautiful Sunday morning, and I had arrived at church early to get a good seat up front. Although I was raised in church, it had only been one year since I had received the baptism of the Holy Spirit, and I was really enjoying going to a church that taught the full gospel message.

While waiting for the service to begin, I was surprised when a woman I didn't even know turned around from the row in front of me and said, "There are angels sitting up in the ceiling on the rafters, and I can see them." Having made that statement she turned back around and kept staring up toward the ceiling of the sanctuary. Although this woman, who was in her mid-forties, was well dressed and seemed very stately in her etiquette, her comment threw me off a bit. My first thought was, "This woman must be a real fruitcake!"

Well, as soon as that thought entered my mind, she turned right back around, held out her hand to me and said, "Here, God told me to give this to you." She placed a twenty dollar bill into my hand and then turned back around just as the pastor was stepping behind the pulpit to begin the service.

After the opening prayer, the church began a time of praise and worship and everyone was having a great time except for me. In my heart I felt so convicted for having judged this woman. Earlier that morning as I drove to church, I was actually wondering how I was going to be able to eat lunch after the service. I was still a few days away from my next payday at work and had run out of money. It dawned on me that because this woman had been sensitive to the Holy Spirit to obey His divine leading through handing me money at a much needed time, then it was most probable to assume that she was also telling the truth about having seen the angels in the church.

As time went by, several leaders in the church told me that the woman sitting in front of me that day was known to spend much time in prayer and was considered to be one of the finest Christians in the church. I repented of my sin of pride and presumption and made a commitment to learn more about what God revealed in his Word concerning His holy angels. One thing is for sure, if we honor the Word of God concerning the ministry of angels then it causes an elevated level of angelic activity to take place in our lives.

God will not intrude in areas where He is not welcomed or invited. If someone disrespects the ministry of the angels then they can expect very little, if any, angelic intervention to take place toward them. It's the same way with all ministries defined in the Bible. If someone thinks that divine healing is a joke and makes fun of preachers who have healing ministries, they are left to tough it out through the limitations of medical science. God loves to heal the sick, but a person has to have faith in Jesus as their Healer in order to receive divine healing and respect His anointed ministers. Let us open our hearts more fully to all that Jesus has made available to us through His angels.

Working with the angels is much like a basketball game. In basketball, everyone on the team needs to be involved. Angels are not slaves who can be bossed around or demanded to do certain things. In the coming chapters, some practical ways will be examined that allow us to biblically work in harmony with the angels assigned to us.

You are on a team whether you know it or not. You are not capable, nor are you expected to win the game all by yourself. It's time to get the angels off the bench and get them into the game with you. However, to work with angels requires spiritual maturity. The following chapters were not

written for the lazy Christian who misplaced his Bible three weeks ago and still doesn't even know it's missing. This book was written as a mandate from God to stir up His end-time champions who will experience some of the greatest exploits ever seen in the history of the world. It requires the utmost discipline, total commitment, and a deep burning passion to walk as closely to God as possible.

Chapter Two

GOD'S HEAVENLY
RANKING ORDER

GOD'S HEAVENLY RANKING ORDER

One of the most important keys to determine in the study of angels is to understand where we, as children of God, stand along with the angels in the category of God's order of rank, or classification. After reading many books and talking with a lot of people about angels, I can tell you that most Christians believe that angels are superior in rank to the children of God.

I understand how some may come to this conclusion if casually reading over only a few Scripture passages that, on the surface, seem to imply this thought. However, we are told in Second Timothy to:

Be diligent to present yourself approved to God, a worker who does not need to be ashamed, rightly dividing the word of truth (2 Timothy 2:15 NKJV).

There is a big difference between studying the Word of God with great diligence and just skimming over the surface, never meditating or pondering on the content.

I'm mindful of the story about the spirited young pastor some time ago who possessed great ministry potential; but he preached himself into a difficult position because of his failure to spend time studying and meditating on the Word of God.

One Sunday morning, this young pastor stood in the pulpit before the congregation and told the people he didn't believe that studying the Bible was really necessary. He said all he needed to do was pray before the meeting, and that he wasn't concerned about what topic he would preach about that day. He figured he would just preach on whatever he opened his Bible to, and then obey anything he read, even if it didn't make sense to him.

To prove his theory, he told the church audience that he was going to randomly open his Bible and let his finger fall on a passage of Scripture. He told them he would do this twice and that he would immediately obey the two Scriptures that were randomly selected. Then, with his eyes closed and the church members watching uneasily, he opened his Bible and the first Scripture that his finger fell on was Matthew 27:5:

...and he departed and went and hanged himself.

The minister said to the audience, which now appeared a bit nervous, "Well, that verse sure is interesting. Let me close my eyes and pick my final Scripture." As he again randomly allowed his Bible to fall open and placed his finger upon a verse, the minister began to break out into a cold sweat as he read the verse out loud which he had committed to obey in accordance with the previous verse he just read. The final verse his finger fell on was Luke 10:37:

Then said Jesus unto him, "Go, and do thou likewise."

As you see by this example, it's important for us to dig beneath the surface and study the clear meaning of what the Lord is conveying to us in His Word and to keep Scripture in its proper context. Psalm 8:4-5 is one such passage. Many believers have not dug deep enough to understand the true meaning. A sincere yet incorrect interpretation of this verse has caused many people to view their relationship with God inaccurately. Let's take a closer look at these often quoted verses:

What is man, that thou art mindful of him? and the son of man, that thou visitest him? For thou hast made him a little lower than the angels, and hast crowned him with glory and honor (Psalm 8:4-5).

When people read this verse they are quick to respond by saying, "See, man is on a lower level than the angels." Yet, even if this does appear to be true, than many other puzzling questions arise, such as, "If angels are superior to man, then why did the apostle Paul say that we would judge angels?"

Do you not know that we shall judge angels...?
(1 Corinthians 6:3 NKJV).

After all, no one has the authority to judge someone who holds a superior position. On occasion, I have watched court cases and each time I was there I saw the exact same scenario played out. The court is called to order; the judge walks into the room. The sheriff says, "All rise!" Everyone in the courtroom stands up to show honor and respect for the judge. The judge does not stand up for the people; the people stand up for him. Then the judge takes his seat, and the proceedings begin. After hearing both sides of the case, and if there is no jury, the judge announces his verdict, brings down his gavel, and his decision is enforced by law.

Of all the times I have been in a courtroom, I have never seen anyone stand up and make judgment against the judge. Why? Because the judge is superior. Should the judge ever need to face judgment, then it requires someone with a higher rank to bring it forth. All things must be done in proper order and rank. We could not judge angels if they were superior to us.

There will come a future occasion in Heaven, after our full redemption is realized, when we will judge angels. Some Bible teachers present the concept that this judging refers to fallen angels, but the Bible does not refer to these angels as being fallen angels.

I believe that in First Corinthians, the apostle Paul is referring to the truth that we will judge the angels that were assigned to us during our earthly life as to how they performed and carried out their responsibilities and duties during their "Tour of Duty." This is a joyful ruling over which we will preside. Honors of distinction, merit, and commendation will be awarded to the angels for faithfully discharging their assigned duties given to them by God. If it appears that man is on a higher level of rank than angels, then what is the Holy Spirit saying through this passage of Scripture in Psalm chapter 8?

It seems to me that when the early translators of the King James Version encountered verse 5 of Psalm chapter 8 they were quite possibly stunned by the literal Hebrew translation. The literal translation of this verse may have been too far beyond their ability to comprehend; therefore, they employed human intervention and changed the wording to something that they deemed to be more "realistic."

This is not the only time this happened to the King James translators. There are other instances of deliberate oversight such as the example in the New Testament regarding the word *baptism*. When the King James translators converted the Greek word *baptism* into the English language, they were faced with the fact that the word *baptism* means to "submerge beneath the water." This was a situation of great concern for them because the common practice of the day regarding baptizing was to sprinkle the person with water.

In order not to disturb their beloved man-made tradition of sprinkling, they simply left the word *baptize* as it was and did not translate it at all. This way, they decided, no one would know that the true meaning of baptism is to submerge beneath the water, and their tradition of sprinkling would go on unchanged.

Let's take a look at a literal translation of Psalm 8:5 and see what the Bible actually says.

> *What is man that You take thought of him? And the son of man that You care for him? Yet You made him a little lower than* **God***, and You crowned him with glory and majesty* (Psalm 8:5 NASB).

In the original Hebrew, it actually says, *"Yet You made him a little lower than* **Elohim***." Elohim* is one of the Hebrew compound names of God. It may be hard for some to grasp this truth, and certainly the King James translators did the best they could with the understanding they had in their day and time while still producing the most trusted translation in existence; but the more one studies the Word of God, the truth becomes quite evident that man was created just a shade lower than God Himself.

This fact should not surprise us because Jesus Himself came into this world as a man. In the beginning, Jesus, the Word, was with God in fellowship and union, and had a separate existence before He came to the earth. He possessed the same nature as God and was equal with God. Yet He took upon Himself the body of a man that He might redeem lost humankind back to God. An unfathomable miracle took place when Jesus left Heaven and was placed by the Holy Spirit in the womb of a young virgin girl named Mary. The Word became flesh—the Incarnation.

God and man became united in one person—Jesus Christ. When Jesus left Heaven to become a man, He did not give up His manhood after 33-1/2 years on the earth. When He died, rose again, and went back to Heaven, He was still a man. He became a man for infinity. Because of the Incarnation, there is a Man in Heaven today at the Father's right hand.

> *For there is one God, and one mediator between God and men,* **the man** *Christ Jesus* (1 Timothy 2:5).

The truth of this high rank granted to man is found not only in verse 5, but also in the following verse when David said:

> *For You made us only a little lower than God, and you crowned us with glory and honor. You put us in charge of everything you made, giving us* **authority** *over all things* (Psalm 8:5-6 NLT).

The subject of authority is another clear indicator of how man is the apex of God's creation. The Lord did not delegate authority over the earth to angels, but rather to men. Even now, while still here on the earth, the Bible tells us that we are seated with Christ in the heavenly realms. The term of being seated is not applied to angels, but to the Lord Jesus and His triumphant church.

> *And God raised us up with the Christ and seated us with Him in the heavenly realms in Christ Jesus...* (Ephesians 2:6 NIV).

It's interesting to note that when you study the Bible you will not read that angels are seated in the presence of God. The angels are standing. We do see in the Book of Revelation that the 24 elders have thrones in which they are seated in a circle around the throne of God; but the 24 elders do not appear to be angels, nor human beings either. They appear to be some other type of spiritual beings that God has specially created.

Redeemed humankind can sit in the presence of God because we are sons and daughters of God, and we are heirs of God and joint heirs with Jesus Christ. A joint heir shares all of his possessions equally with the one he is joined to. A respected minister of the Gospel named Peter Tan prayed to God for many years to see the glorious wonders of Heaven. When God answered his prayer and took him to Heaven in 1994, one of the things the Lord showed him while he was there was the throne room of God.

As Peter Tan wept before the Lord due to the overwhelming wonder and splendor of His majesty, he was caught off guard when the Lord Jesus stepped out from His throne and invited him to sit on it. Peter Tan was shocked and so startled that he could hardly speak. Even though Brother Tan was familiar with the Scripture about being seated with Christ in heavenly places, it was hard for him to imagine how real the full meaning of this verse actually was when confronted with the reality of it. He explains how the tremendous awe of being invited to sit on the throne was almost more than he could take, but the Lord held his hand and placed him on His throne.

Brother Tan describes his experience of sitting on the throne as one of entering into infinity, where time ceases to exist. The verbalized power of the living Word of God is so awesome, that once it is spoken, there is nothing in heaven or earth that can stop it from coming to pass.

There is a difference between our relationship with God and the relationship that angels have with God. The Bible says that:

> *It was revealed to them [the prophets] that they were not serving themselves but you, when they spoke of the things that have now been told you by those who have preached the gospel to you by the Holy Spirit sent from heaven.* ***Even angels long to look into these things*** (1 Peter 1:12 NIV).

Angels have a great interest and fascination with the salvation message and the new birth experience. The great interest is generated by the mystery of what it must be like to be born again. After all, an angel cannot be born again because that is not an option God gave them. None of the former preachers who have died and have now gone to Heaven are walking along the streets of gold, preaching to the angels and trying to get the angels saved. Angels were not created by God to experience the redemption plan. In Heaven, the angels praise and worship God with singing, but they cannot sing the "Song of the Redeemed," because they are not able to experience the redemption process. They are already pure and holy.

This is why lucifer was condemned for all eternity the moment he rebelled against God and was ejected from Heaven, along with one third of the angels who foolishly went with him. Lucifer, whose name was changed to satan, did not have a legal right to do his own thing. He was created to serve as a powerful, covering cherub, and the moment he became discontent with his assigned position, he was already on the way out.

A key difference between humans and angels is the fact that God gave us a free will. The remaining two-thirds of angels that stayed behind in Heaven to obey God were the ones who realized they did not even have the right to leave. It wasn't an option for them to give their opinion or express their viewpoint. This is why satan's judgment to burn in the lake of fire and brimstone for all eternity is final and will never be revoked.

Recently, I was talking with an elderly Christian man who said the Lord appeared to him earlier in his life and offered him a call to the ministry office of the prophet along with a special anointing to stand in that ministry office. Because this Christian brother had seen the abuse and mistreatment that a well-known prophet had received by fellow Christians, he responded to the Lord by saying, "No, Lord, I'd rather not." I asked him how the Lord reacted to his negative response. He said the Lord was noticeably displeased and said, "You mean you don't want my gift?" The dear brother's final response to the Lord was, "Actually, Lord, I'd rather have something else."

In my heart I felt so saddened when he said that to the Lord, knowing that many people choose to take the path in life that offers the most comfort instead of the high calling of God. The

statement is certainly true that "many are called, but few are chosen." (Matt. 22:14). This man was called by God as a prophet, but he chose not to step into the specific ministry destined for him because of the challenges he would have to face.

What's amazing about the God we serve is that He will actually honor the choices we make, even if they are not His best plans for our lives. Of course, the Christian who does not follow the Lord's plan for his life will have to endure the judgment of those poorly made choices when he stands before the Judge of the universe. Some believer's will make it to Heaven, but will enter with absolutely no rewards because they chose to do their own thing in life. Paul encouraged us to work out our own salvation with fear and trembling. (see Phil. 2:12). This is why it is so important to spend time with God in prayer and seek *His* plan for your life.

ANGELS AND HEBREWS

As we move into the New Testament, we see the writer of Hebrews expounding on Psalm chapter 8 and shedding new light on the passage. The Bible does not tell us who wrote the Book of Hebrews. I have heard biblical scholars suggest who they think wrote the Book of Hebrews. A minister on the radio thought the scholarly Apollos wrote Hebrews because the style of the original Greek writing was similar to Paul's style.

I think it is interesting when divine revelation is given regarding certain Bible subjects. Sometimes, extra-biblical truths can be shared by the Lord in the present day era in which we live. There is a difference between extra-biblical and unbiblical. If a teaching is unbiblical, then we need to dismiss it and stay away from it. However, if it is extra-biblical then we can judge it by comparing it with the written Word of God, as well as judging whether or not it bears witness with our spirit.

Reverend Kenneth E. Hagin said that during a visitation from the Lord he asked the Lord, "Who wrote the Book of Hebrews?" He said the Lord told him that, "Paul did." Actually, there was no one else who had the revelation knowledge that Paul possessed. He was the only one qualified to write the Book of Hebrews. Most of the other apostles were not as quick to absorb the truth that Jesus wanted to redeem all humankind, not just the Jewish race.

It's important to note that you can't figure out spiritual truths with natural, logical thinking. Many people try to understand Scripture by applying analytical and rational evaluation, but they fail to understand this great truth: *You do not contact God with your brain; you contact God with your spirit.*

God is a Spirit, and He must be worshiped in spirit and truth. (see John 4:24). That's why the person who is filled with a greater measure of the Spirit of God most often walks in a greater level of understanding of the Word of God. Jesus said:

> *...the words I have spoken to you are spirit, and they are life* (John 6:63 NIV).

It is not necessary for you to know the Hebrew or Greek language to know God. As a child of God, the Holy Spirit lives inside of you, and He will guide you into all truth. It is spiritual enlightenment that makes one see more clearly, not necessarily earning a Ph.D. in Theology. I've met quite a few people with college degrees, yet they generated little spiritual heat. Having a degree doesn't mean it comes with anointing or heavenly power. God's people should not place too much value in titles and degrees, but rather keep the gospel simple and uncluttered, as the Lord meant it to be.

Let's look at the prophecy about Jesus from Psalm 8 that Paul now expounds upon in the Book of Hebrews.

> *But one has testified somewhere, saying; What is man that you remember him? Or the son of man that you are concerned about him? You have made him **for a little while** lower than the angels, you have crowned him with glory and honor, and have appointed him over the works of your hands, you have put all things in subjection under his feet* (Hebrews 2:6-8 NASB).

Paul was writing to those he knew were familiar with the Old Testament Scriptures, so he only needed to give a general reference without mentioning the author, which was David the psalmist, and the Scripture quoted is Psalm 8:4-6. The thrust of what Paul brings out from Psalm 8 is that dominion was clearly given to man. However, man lost that dominion through sin.

For Old Testament saints, it would not have occurred to them that this Psalm was referring to the coming Messiah, who would win back what the first Adam lost. For an Old Testament saint, Psalm 8 simply revealed man's authority to rule the earth that God had originally given to man. But the authority was lost when Adam committed high treason and sold out to the devil in the Garden of Eden.

When David wrote Psalm 8 only a shadow of that former glory remained upon humankind, of which Adam originally walked in, even though man in his fallen nature still bore resemblances of the appeal of God. Paul brings to light that David focused on man in Psalm 8, while at the same time he understood that David was a prophet and David foresaw "a man" who would rule with all things being placed under His feet.

This man that David prophesied about was, of course, the Lord Jesus Christ, who became the second Adam to win back what the first Adam lost. So, this Scripture actually has a dual meaning. First, man was made a little lower than God and was created to have dominion over the earth. Second, Jesus, for a little while during His earthly ministry, was made a little lower than the angels; but now He has been raised back up as the Lord of Heaven and earth, and He has raised us up to rule and reign with Him.

So even if you feel inferior to an angel now, it is only temporary, because a child of God is eternally superior, just as Jesus Himself is superior to all angels. When we step over into glory and realize our full redemption, then the awesome fullness of who we are in Christ will be completely known.

Angels are not referred to in Scripture as "brethren," but we as saints of the Most High God are His brethren. Jesus is actually our Elder Brother because He was the first to rise from the dead, and we have been raised up with Him.

> *For whom He foreknew, He also predestined to be conformed to the image of His Son, that He might be the **firstborn among many brethren*** (Romans 8:29 NKJV).

What a special privilege and sense of distinction it is to be a member of God's family and to have Jesus as our Elder Brother. It's important to note that angels are not referred to in the Bible as sons and daughters of God, yet we as His redeemed saints are His children. It's impossible for angels to be sons and daughters of God, because they do not meet a required biblical mandate that we see in the following verse:

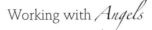

*Because God's children are human beings—**made of flesh and blood**—Jesus also became flesh and blood by being born in human form. For only as a human being could He die, and only by dying could he break the power of the Devil, who had the power of death (Hebrews 2:14 NLT).*

Please notice the phrase, *"Because God's children are human beings—made of flesh and blood."* To be a human being made of flesh and blood is a requirement necessary to be a child of God. Angels do not meet this requirement because angels are pure spirit beings, not possessing a physical body.

*And of the angels He says: Who makes His angels **spirits** And His ministers a flame of fire (Hebrews 1:7 NKJV).*

ANGELS AND JOB

What about the sons of God in Job 38:7? One time, I was asked a very good question about the "sons of God" mentioned in the Book of Job, which many people believe to be in reference to angels. This would, of course, seem to imply that the angels are referred to as God's sons. To better understand the phrase mentioned in Job, let's examine how the same term is used in Genesis.

*Now it came to pass, that when men began to multiply on the face of the earth, and daughters were born to them, that the **sons of God** saw the **daughters of men**, that they were beautiful, and they took wives for themselves of all whom they chose (Genesis 6:1-2 NKJV).*

This is the first mention in the Bible of "sons of God and daughters of men." Some Christians view this verse as implying that the disobedient angels who were kicked out of Heaven came down and took human women as wives and through sexual relations produced the race of giants known as the Nephilim.

This interpretation does not fit for several reasons. First, verse 3 clearly identifies who the "sons of God" are:

And the LORD said, My Spirit shall not strive with **man** *forever, for he is indeed flesh,* **yet his days shall be one hundred and twenty years** (Genesis 6:3 NKJV).

The sons of God mentioned in verse 2 are identified in verse 3 as being *men* who strive against the Spirit of God. The context is clearly about men who failed to walk closely with God, and not about angels. The sons of God refer to the natural descendants of Seth who were godly men, yet they succumbed to carnal desires and began to marry ungodly women. These women are identified as the "daughters of men," which refers to those women who were descendants of Cain, the man who murdered his brother.

Genesis chapters 4 and 5 trace the expansion of the human race through two primary, yet different lines, directed by Cain and Seth. It was extremely displeasing to God that these men from a godly lineage were intermarrying with ungodly women just because they were physically attractive.

Because the Holy Spirit found it so difficult to work with men who consistently proved so unfaithful, He set a time boundary upon man's lease upon the earth. The earth is the Lord's, and the fullness thereof, and although he has given man authority over the earth, the Lord is still the owner of this planet that we live on (see Ps. 24:1, Gen. 1:28).

There have been numerous documented cases of people living to be well over 120 years of age. So, the Scripture here is not saying that no one will ever live longer than 120 years of age; it is simply referring to jubilee years, which are each represented by a period of 50 years. Multiplying 120 years times 50 jubilee years totals 6,000 years. I believe that after 6,000 years of human activity on this earth is completed, man's lease on planet Earth expires, and the Lord Jesus will reign supreme—wicked men will be subdued by the Lord's system of government where He rules with a rod of iron.

> *There were **giants** [Hebrew: Nephilim] on the earth in those days, and also afterward, when the sons of God came into the daughters of men and they bore children to them. Those were the mighty men who were of old, men of renown* (Genesis 6:4 NKJV).

As mentioned earlier, some Christians understand this verse as saying that the sons of God were fallen angels who had sexual relations with earthly women and thus produced a race of giants. Yet, the sons of God being mentioned once again are men; and the problem that God was having with man is the subject of Genesis 6:1-7.

Angels are not mentioned in this Scripture passage, and it would be a guess to imply otherwise. It's also interesting to consider that the Scripture in Genesis 6:2 says the sons of God *took wives* for themselves from the daughters of men. Personally, I have never known the devil to believe in marriage. The devil loves destroying marriages, and he promotes immorality. No fallen angel is going to take a wife because the devil has no respect for the sanctity of marriage. People often wonder then about how giants were produced if not through some form of superhuman, demonic intervention.

Everything back in Adam's time was big. The dinosaurs were huge, the trees were gigantic, even insects such as dragonflies were enormous compared to today's insects. During the time before the flood, the earth was contained within a natural, hyperbaric (extremely heavy and protective) biosphere, and everything in it grew to incredible size. In museums, I've seen fossils of ancient sharks that make today's Great White shark look like a small catfish. It would be unrealistic to think that this environment did not somehow affect Adam and Eve. Adam and Eve must have certainly been sized in proportion so as not to be at a disadvantage.

Even after sin entered the world and the great flood destroyed much of the original life extending benefits that were in the earth, there was still a carry-over effect that lasted hundreds of years. Consequently, I don't believe a fallen angel was involved in some act of perversion to create a giant offspring. After all, Adam was big, powerful, had a genius mind, and was well able to defend himself in a world that included some heavy-duty predators.

I also find it difficult to accept the idea that Genesis 6 is referring to fallen angels that had relations with women and produced giants, because regarding marriage in Heaven, Jesus said:

> *At the resurrection people will neither marry nor be given in marriage,* **they will be like the angels in heaven** (Matthew 22:30 NIV).

Since angels do not marry, this verse also implies that neither are they capable of sexual reproduction. The angels in Heaven can be male or female, but they are not capable of sexual reproduction, and neither will we when we get there. Some people think there are only male angels because of the mention of Michael and Gabriel in the Bible. But I believe that there are millions upon millions of holy angels in God's Kingdom, consisting of both male and female angels. Just as the human race includes male and female, so does the angelic race include male and female. This is why we are told in the Book of Hebrews to be hospitable and kind to strangers, because some people who have done this have entertained angels without knowing it! Angels can present themselves in concealed forms of men or women, thus disguising their true identity.

I don't believe a fallen angel is able to relate sexually with a woman and produce a child. Of course, I do understand that through immoral acts people can yield themselves to demonic influences and aide the devil when it comes to perpetuating an ungodly lineage. But that is not to say that the devil can duplicate a virgin birth. It takes the natural seed of a man to impregnate a woman, which is why the virgin Mary giving birth to our Lord Jesus was a divine miracle of God. Even if we supposed that fallen angels had relations with ungodly women and produced giants, then why don't we see this take place today? Certainly if the devil was successful with this tactic once, then he would implement this plan consistently and there would be giants among us today. These ideas about angels relating with women are nothing more than myths based on traditional Gnosticism. They need to be dismissed just like the silly ideas of Greek mythology which taught that the gods had relations with humans and produced individuals like Hercules, etc.

I understand that some say the Book of Enoch supports this teaching about fallen angels having relations with women on earth, and that the result were giants that walked the earth, but that is misguided information. While the Book of Enoch does offer some interesting insight into spiritual matters and is even referenced in the Holy Bible by Jude, it is, however, admitted by all critical writers and thinkers, that the Book of Enoch contains contradictory legends concerning the fall and the judgment of the angels. The passage regarding the fallen angels relating with women says that giants were produced that were 900 feet tall.

While we are aware of individuals such as Goliath and other giants that measured around 12 feet in height, giants that are 900 feet tall is cause for skepticism. The Book of Enoch is also comprised of earlier and latter materials; and the section mentioning angel marriages, without any uncertainty belongs to the so-called book of *Noah*, which, I believe, is a fictitious and totally unreliable book.

In Job 38:7, we see the dual meaning of the phrase "sons of God." In this context, the Lord is asking Job where he was when creation events took place.

> *When the morning stars sang together, and all the **sons of God** shouted for joy?* (Job 38:7 KJV).

In this Scripture passage, it is quite clear that the sons of God being mentioned are angels—not humans because they were not yet created. The angels were rejoicing because God had laid the earth's cornerstone, and it was a moment to celebrate as a new world that would be home for the human race was being established. It is important to distinguish between the context of how the phrase *sons of God* is used, and to determine whether the reference is to men or angels. Often times, it refers only to angels, but that is not always the case as we saw in Genesis chapter 6.

This then raises the question of whether or not angels are literal sons of God, as Jesus is the Son of God the Father. It would appear that the angels are called *the sons of God* because they are created by Him, and they serve Him as a son serves his father. However, angels are not "sons" as is the Everlasting Son. They are called sons by God's grace and favor, revealing His awesome love for them.

Man has always been and always will be the supreme creation of God because out of all creatures and beings in Heaven and on earth, only man is found to be in the god classification. The apostle Paul wrote:

> *The **god** of this age has blinded the minds of unbelievers, so that they cannot see the light of the gospel of the glory of Christ, who is the image of God* (2 Corinthians 4:4 NIV).

Adam was created by God to be the god over this world. Notice that Adam is identified as being a god (not G-o-d), there is only one big God, and we all know who He is. The One True God we love and worship is God the Father, God the Son, (who is the Lord Jesus Christ), and God the Holy Spirit.

Adam was given authority to govern this planet, but disaster took place when Adam committed high treason and sold out to the devil. Satan took the authority that Adam originally had, and the devil still has authority over the world system and unbelievers today. When Jesus came to the earth He destroyed the power of the devil and triumphed over all the forces of darkness through His death, burial, and triumphant resurrection. What Adam lost, Jesus won back by becoming the second Adam who was able to defeat the devil by living a sinless life as a man.

Today, any born-again believer in Christ has been transferred out of the kingdom of darkness and now resides in the glorious Kingdom of light. The authority that Adam lost has been restored in Christ and is now available for everyone who receives Jesus as their Lord and Savior. Man's honor, rank, and dignity have been restored by the Lord Jesus Christ. Jesus Himself referred to the truth that man is in the *god classification*.

> *Jesus answered them, "Is it not written in your law,* **'I have said you are gods?'"** (John 10:34 NIV).

If He called them *"gods,"* to whom the Word of God came—and the Scripture cannot be broken—what about the one whom the Father set apart as His very own and sent into the world?

Some choose to believe that the gods being mentioned here by Jesus refers to angels, but that can't be, because in referring to the gods, Jesus said the Word of God came to *them*, which refers to men. The Word of God never came to angels; it came to men through preaching. The religious leaders were outraged at Jesus because He declared that He was God's Son. They understood that His declaration actually put Him on the same level as God, and they accused Him of blasphemy.

> *Why then do you accuse me of blasphemy because I said,* "I am God's Son? (John 10:36b NIV).

Today, some Christians would be quick to label another believer as a heretic if they thought that person actually believed they were a god. Some Christians have such a low opinion of their identity in Christ that they would consider it blasphemy for another Christian brother or sister to think they are a god. Sadly enough, though, some unsaved sinners involved in New Age practices realize that each person has ingrained God-attributes in them. After all, eternity is contained within the heart of every person.

Based on a person's choice regarding the Lord Jesus, everyone is going to spend eternity either in Heaven or in the lake that burns with fire and brimstone. Eternal life is what awaits the child of God, with a future that is so vast and glorious that it will take forever to tap into the endless joys that await us.

My friend, it will take someone who is in a god classification that possesses eternal life, in order to explore the billions upon billions of star systems, galaxies, nebulae's, and other hidden wonders throughout the universe that God has prepared for those who love Him. This earth life is just a training ground for ruling and reigning for all eternity. While this may stretch one's ability to comprehend the exhaustless limits of God's goodness toward us (it sure does mine!), we can still, for now, sense in our eternal spirits what so quickly goes beyond our natural understanding. Because Jesus redeemed us, we have become divine partakers of the nature of God as we continue to grow and mature in Him.

> *For by these He has granted to us His precious and magnificent promises, so that by them* **you may become partakers of the divine nature,** *having escaped the corruption that is in the world by lust* (2 Peter 1:4 NASB).

There is an element of divinity that resides in a child of God. The divine nature of God has been imparted to us within our hearts. Humankind is special; and we should always be thanking our God for the awesome relationship that we have with Him through Jesus, our Lord. The prophet Jeremiah learned the same lesson from God, as the Lord revealed to him how to leave behind spiritual sluggishness, and run at full speed with the horses.

Running with
the Horses

Running with
the Horses

The prophet Jeremiah was very open in his relationship with the Lord. When times were tough for him, he did not pretend like it didn't bother him. Jeremiah always pleaded his case with God. Through prayer, he would contend with the Lord over the difficult problems which he faced in his day and age.

In Jeremiah chapter 12, we see the frustration that Jeremiah experienced through not understanding the patience and love of God. Jeremiah wanted to see God bring swift judgment to rebellious Israel, but in his own discontentment he failed to realize how heartbroken the Lord was over His chosen people who had rejected Him.

Lord, you always give me justice when I bring a case before you. Now let me bring you this complaint: Why are

the wicked so prosperous? Why are evil people so happy? You have planted them, and they have taken root and prospered. Your name is on their lips, but in their hearts they give you no credit at all. But as for me, LORD, you know my heart. You see me and test my thoughts. Drag these people away like helpless sheep to be butchered! Set them aside to be slaughtered! How long must this land weep? Even the grass in the fields has withered. The wild animals and birds have disappeared because of the evil in the land. Yet, the people have said, The Lord doesn't see what's ahead for us! (Jeremiah 12:1-4 NLT).

Often times, we see in Scripture that God's prophets were faced with heavy discouragement that was sent from the devil in an attempt to steal their joy and expectancy. The same temptation was faced by Elijah, who, during a time of intense backlash from the enemy, thought he was the only one serving God in all of Israel. Yet, God encouraged him telling him that He had reserved 7,000 faithful followers who had never bowed their knees to Baal (see 1 Kings 19:18).

Jeremiah had allowed himself to slip into a mind-set of comparing his own spiritual condition with the spiritual corruption so prevalent around him. Jeremiah actually thought he was doing pretty good spiritually compared to the majority of Israel. However, comparing yourself with others is not an accurate way to determine genuine spiritual maturity. It can be very misleading when you think you are at the pinnacle of holiness just because you do not smoke or chew tobacco. I've met people in the church that thought they had attained the highest levels of pleasing God, yet all they were demonstrating was pride and a religious spirit because they thought their denomination was superior.

We live in a church age when many believer's love to talk about in-vogue topics, such as: intimacy with God, abiding in His presence, and experiencing the glory realm. While many people discuss these wonderful topics, many never really carry out the plan or demonstrate the walk. Much personal loss occurs for Christians when we fail to enter into the rich inheritance that Jesus purchased for us at the Cross.

This loss is not the same kind as that of failing to follow through with an exercise plan, or giving up on the new diet that promised a slim waistline. What is lost is the opportunity to attain the Promised Land that God destined for each of His children to possess. To enter the land of promise requires a living faith in God, and it takes diligence in prayer and time in the Word to keep faith alive when circumstances and natural elements oppose the promises of God.

Sometimes, the Lord has to speak to us just as He did to Jeremiah about getting the slack out of our lives. I like how Jeremiah not only recorded the prophetic words that God had him speak to Israel, but also the prophetic words that God spoke to him as an individual, even the ones that brought correction. The Lord lovingly shared some things with Jeremiah that specifically addressed his over-inflated ego. The Lord said:

> ***"If racing against mere men makes you tired, how will you race against horses?*** *If you stumble and fall on open ground, what will you do in the thickets near the Jordan?"* (Jeremiah 12:5 NLT).

To run with horses implies going to a higher level. In order to go to a higher level, we must first have revelation of just where we are in our walk with God, and then be willing to stretch farther to ascend into new realms.

Over a decade ago, when I practiced martial arts, I was sparring one day with a fiend of mine a well-known black belt in Tae Kwon Do. Although we had often talked, I had never trained one-on-one or sparred with him. He was about ten years older than I, and he had competed in many tournaments against others who had different martial art styles. He had even competed against the heavyweight Tae Kwon Do Olympic Gold Medalist. Because of his experience, I was looking forward to learning as much as possible from him.

As we met at the dojang (Tae Kwon Do training center) for a sparring session, I was determined to make a respectable showing of what I had learned over the years. He and I both trained under the same Master Instructor from Korea, but we did not see each other very often because he was in the military and traveled a great deal of the time. That day proved to be an important learning session for me. Once the sparring began, it was only about ten minutes before the fighting became very intense. Our uniforms were soaked with sweat, and I was going all out just trying to hold my ground without loosing any teeth in the process.

He paused just for a moment, and with his breathing much more controlled then mine, said, "Now we are going to take it to another level." The fighting resumed, and I realized very quickly that I was in over my head. Fortunately, he embodied the true spirit of a martial artist because he pulled most of his kicks before making contact. I had seen him fight before, and he wasn't as gracious with other opponents. He wasn't out to show off by knocking me out cold on the floor, but rather he was making it painfully clear what skills and techniques were needed to move up to the level of a highly proficient martial artist.

Today, the Holy Spirit wants to open the eyes of our heart and help us realize that there are much greater dimensions of majesty and glory to be found in Jesus, the Anointed One. *To run with horses* requires supernatural empowerment. No person can naturally match the speed of a horse in full gallop; but when the Holy Spirit comes upon us in power, we can run like Elijah when he outran King Ahab's chariot being pulled by the nation's fastest horses.

To run with the horses, requires an accurate appraisal of just where we stand in our relationship with God. The legendary apostle to India in the early 19th century, Sadhu Sundar Singh, had an interesting experience when the Lord Jesus allowed him to be taken to Heaven. On one occasion during his frequent heavenly visions, Brother Singh saw angels escorting newly arriving saints into an intermediate level in Heaven. As Brother Singh watched, he noticed a pastor who had just died on the earth being escorted into Heaven by several angels. As the pastor was taken to the intermediate level in heaven, he noticed another man who had also just arrived in Heaven, being taken to a higher position. The pastor immediately protested to the angels, saying, "Why is he being taken to a higher level than me? Neither in holiness nor anything else, am I in any way less than this man!"

The angels responded to him that this man had gained this position by his godly life and his faith. They explained to the pastor that he was not prepared to go to a higher level, and that he would have to stay at this low intermediate level until he had been taught essential lessons which were not learned on earth. At hearing this, the pastor said, "I have been teaching people all my life about the way to reach Heaven. What more have I to learn? I know all about it."

Then the instructing angels said, "They must go up now, we can't detain them, but we will answer your question. My friend, do not be offended if we speak plainly, for it is for your good. You think you are alone here, but the Lord is also here though you cannot see Him. The pride that you displayed when you said, "I know all about it" prevents you from seeing Him, and from going up higher. Humility is the cure for this pride. Practice it and your desire will be granted."

After this, one of the angels told him, "The man who has just been promoted above you, was no learned or famous man. You did not look at him very carefully. He was a member of your own congregation. People hardly knew him at all, for he was an ordinary working man, and had little leisure from his work. But in his workshop, many knew him as an industrious and honest worker. All who came in contact with him recognized his Christian character.

"In the war, he was called up for service in France. There, one day, as he was helping a wounded comrade, he was struck by a bullet and killed. Though his death was sudden, he was ready for it, so he did not have to remain in the intermediate state as long as you will have to. His promotion depends, not on favoritism, but on his spiritual worthiness. His life of prayer and humility, while he was in the world, prepared him to a great extent for the spiritual world. Now he is rejoicing at having reached his appointed place, and is thanking and praising the Lord, who, in His mercy has saved him, and given him eternal life."

GETTING SERIOUS

There is becoming an increasingly larger gap between those who really mean business about their relationship with God and those who are just playing religious games. God's people are waking up with a hunger for the meat of His Word, having grown tired of being fed milk for such a long period of time. There is a greater level of discernment flowing through the children of God more then ever before, causing God's holy people to distinguish the difference between slick marketing tactics and the anointing, between hype and genuine Holy Spirit stimulation. As we draw nearer to God, grey areas diminish and things become much more black and white.

Through the Lord's exhortation to Jeremiah, Jeremiah refocuses on his calling and is refueled to prophesy the Word of the Lord. Just as Jeremiah pleaded his case with God, the Lord answered by pleading His case with Jeremiah and challenging him to pick up the pace. This stirred Jeremiah to stop comparing himself with others and to simply focus on being as close to the Lord as possible—being faithful with the prophetic ministry entrusted to him.

WALKING CLOSELY
WITH GOD

━━━━━━━━━━━━━━━━━━━━━━━━━━━━━━━━━━━━━

WALKING CLOSELY
WITH GOD

To run with the horses, as Jeremiah discovered, takes a level of dedication and commitment that goes beyond what is considered "normal" Christianity. What most people consider "normal" is often a very low level of spirituality, where it is sometimes difficult to even distinguish whether or not a person is saved.

Before the Lord placed me in full-time ministry, I had a good job at one of the top home improvement stores in America. While working, I always strived to be one of the best employees in the store. Through the blessing of the Lord, coupled with hard work, I became not only my department's top sales specialist, but also the top salesman for our district of ten stores located in a very competitive Southern California market.

Even though I worked a full day, I always made sure I maintained quality time with the Lord in personal prayer and Bible study. During my breaks and lunch time, I would often read my Bible, especially in the employee break room. Sometimes people would ask me what I was reading, and I would tell them I was reading the Bible. My response would almost always prompt a conversation about the Lord Jesus, and I was able to witness to many people.

Everybody, including the entire management team, respected me as a minister. Not only because of my conduct and Christian witness, but especially because I worked so hard that when the day came when I stepped over into the ministry fulltime, they hired three people to fill my position.

During the time I worked there, it was amazing how many people came up to me when no one else was around and shared that they, too, were Christians. Honestly, if they had not told me, I would have never guessed that some of them were born again. Many confided in me that they were living in sinful relationships or not going to church, but they truly wanted to serve the Lord. I always poured encouragement into them to follow the Lord, and admonished them to get connected with a local church.

We need to let our light shine, and also give no reason for offense to the gospel. (see Matt. 5:16, 2 Cor. 6:3). By the time I left that job, there were fellow employees who were asking me to answer Bible questions for them; for several of them I had interpreted dreams that they had received from the Lord but did not understand. Others affectionately referred to me as *the priest*, or *the man of the cloth*, or *the preacher man*. I've always believed that ministry should be a by-product of an overflow of God gushing out of us through having an intimate relationship with Him. Certainly, the Lord knows those who are close to Him, and that is the heart of what Christianity is all about.

WALKING AND RUNNING

To increase to a heavenly pace and run with the horses, it is vital to walk closely with the Lord. John G. Lake, the apostle to Africa in the early 1900s and a man who preached divine healing with a passion, wrote about the time he spoke with a woman whom he considered to be one of the most spiritually advanced persons he had ever met. Most people had never heard of her, but yet she made a deep impression upon Dr. Lake.

He said that one day this woman said to him, "Dr. Lake, the Lord Jesus came into my home and sat at my kitchen table with me, and He answered every question that I've ever wanted to ask Him."

Dr Lake said, "Oh, is that right?" He then took a pen and paper and wrote down some questions on the sheet of paper. He handed the paper to this dear lady and said, "Here, next time you see Him, please give this to Him." And with that reply he went back to his work at hand.

Several weeks went by and Dr. Lake saw the woman walking toward him from a distance. He couldn't help but notice that there was a sheet of paper in her hand. She walked up to him with a smile and handed him the paper which contained the list of questions that Dr. Lake had wanted to ask the Lord. As he began to read the answers on the paper, he raised his hands in the air and exclaimed, "Truly, there is no way anyone could have written this, but the Lord."

My friend, the relationship that this woman had is the kind of relationship that God desires for all of His people to have.

Several years ago, an internationally well-known and seasoned minister who lives overseas had a visitation from the Lord, and during his conversation with the Lord, he took the opportunity to inquire about how he could walk more closely with God, much like Enoch did. He said this question greatly pleased the Lord Jesus, so the Lord actually shared with him the names of five people who were closest to Him. The minister said that he did not recognize a single one of them! He had never heard of them before. He said the Lord told him that these five people had actually gotten so close to Him that their appearances began to resemble that of the angels.

The minister gave me just enough information about the people Jesus mentioned, that I went home and searched the Internet. I was able to identify one of the five—a pastor who had a worldwide ministry, yet I had never heard of him. He was in his seventies and his countenance was so holy and pure, he looked like an angel!

It's time to run with the horses and leave mediocrity far behind. We must be willing to gird ourselves up and lay behind sin and the entanglements of this world that would hold us back from a deeper walk with God. The famous missionary to the American Indians, David Brainard, made an interesting statement in his autobiography, in which he said that in his lifetime, he wanted to be the one who is closest to the Lord in his generation. The Lord knows exactly where each person stands in relationship with Himself. He desires for all of us to be near to His heart.

In the Book of Numbers, we see Moses having attained a special place in the eyes of God.

Now Moses was a very humble man, more humble than anyone else on the face of the earth (Numbers 12:3 NIV).

Humility is important to God, and God knew that Moses was the most humble man on the earth during that time. What's remarkable is that Moses is the one who wrote the Book of Numbers. He obviously knew he was the most humble man because the Lord must have told him. Today, the Lord also knows who the most humble person on the earth is. God keeps all sorts of statistics that are of value in His sight. The Lord also keeps financial statistics.

In the land of Uz there lived a man whose name was Job. This man was blameless and upright, he feared God and shunned evil. He had seven sons and three daughters, and he owned seven thousand sheep, three thousand camels, five hundred yoke of oxen and five hundred donkeys, and had a large number of servants. He was the greatest man among all the people of the East (Job 1:1-3 NIV).

Since God was aware that Job was the greatest (richest) man of the east, then God also knew who was the greatest person in the north, south, and west. God knows where each person stands in all facets of life, and He doesn't mind if we prosper financially as long as we avoid covetousness and keep Him the center of our life.

Jesus also recognized the various levels of intimacy that were found among His chosen twelve apostles. All twelve were near to Jesus, but you see the distinction in intimacy clearly revealed during exceptional circumstances.

> *After six days Jesus took with him Peter, James and John the brother of James, and led them up a high mountain by themselves. There he was transfigured before them. His face shone like the sun, and his clothes became as white as the light. Just then there appeared before them Moses and Elijah, talking with Jesus* (Matthew 17:1-3 NIV).

Here we see that out of the twelve apostles, Jesus took the three who were closest to Him to behold His transfiguration on the mountain. I'm sure Jesus wanted to take the others, but He knew that Peter, James, and John were the only ones who were close enough to Him to be able to grasp and appreciate this sacred experience. This event even stretched Peter, James, and John beyond anything they had previously witnessed, causing them to esteem the Lord more highly than ever before. Still, we see an even more intimate fellowship attained by one of the twelve.

> *Near the cross of Jesus stood his mother, his mother's sister, Mary the wife of Clopas, and Mary Magdalene. When Jesus saw his mother there, **and the disciple whom he loved standing nearby**, he said to his mother, "Dear woman, here is your son," and to the disciple, "Here is your mother." From that time on, this disciple took her into his home* (John 19:25-27 NIV).

The amazing love that Jesus had for John is specifically mentioned in Scripture due to the fact that Jesus was aware that John longed for the closest possible relationship with Him. Those who are close to the Lord can be trusted with what is precious to God. The Lord Jesus replaced His physical absence and departure as a son to Mary by positioning John to fill the gap for Mary after He was gone. He also made sure His mother would be taken care of by assigning John to receive Mary as his own mother. You certainly don't entrust your mother to just anybody.

There is another indication in Scripture revealing how attached John was to the Lord.

> *Then Peter, turning around, saw* **the disciple whom Jesus loved** *following, who also had leaned on his breast at the supper, and said, Lord, who is the one who betrays you?* (John 21:20 NKJV).

Here again we see John being referred to as the *disciple whom Jesus loved*. Although John wrote this Gospel, he knew he had special favor with the Lord, just as Moses knew that he was the most humble man on the earth. John even leaned on the Lord's breast which represents a completely open relationship based on genuine love and trust. Because John's relationship with the Lord was closer than that of the other eleven, he was able to directly ask the Lord a question that the others were hesitant to bring up. The others were distressed because the Lord said one of them was going to betray Him.

> *Greatly distressed, one by one they began to ask him, "I'm not the one, am I?* (Mark 14:19 NLT).

The sincerity and purity of the apostles, not including Judas, is seen here, when they don't blame each other, but purge themselves by asking the Lord if it could be one of them. It was Peter who suggested to John that he ask the Lord, because of the loving favor that John had with Jesus. The Scriptures suggest that the Lord whispered to John that it was the one to whom he would pass the sop of bread. After Jesus told John, the others still didn't know that the traitor was Judas. When Judas got up to leave, the others thought he

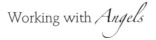

was going to buy food for the feast or take money to the poor; therefore, they must not have heard what Jesus whispered to John. (see John 13:23-30). To hear the secrets that the Lord desires to reveal requires someone who leans closely on the Lord, because you have to be close to hear what is being whispered to you.

We can be as close to the Lord as we want to be. The choice is ours. We can either lean in on the Lord like John did, or be foolish and waste time being engaged in unfulfilling entertainment and games. Now is the time to step up and be a real man or woman of God. *To run with the horses* means to walk closely with God on a consistent basis.

THE SLIPSTREAM

OF HEAVEN

THE SLIPSTREAM
OF HEAVEN

It would be an injustice if I simply told you to run with the horses and walk with God, but did not show you how. In this chapter, I will completely erase the mystery about how to live in a place where you continually experience the presence of God. I'm not one to build a spiritual air castle and then tell people to go live in it when I don't know how to do it myself. This is where good intentions and wishful thinking are separated from daily reality.

If you are ready to run with the horses, let's take a look at a key Scripture passage which serves as a foundation that allows us to coexist in the heavenly and natural realm simultaneously. Our story picks up with the king of Aram sending a large army to capture Elisha. The king of Aram was furious because someone kept informing the king of Israel where he was setting up his military command posts. The king of Aram knew that only his top officers were aware of his battle strategies, so he suspected one of his top men of being a traitor, and was prepared to deal with the situation.

> *This enraged the king of Aram. He summoned his officers and demanded of them, "Will you not tell me which of us is on the side of Israel?" "None of us, my lord the king," said one of his officers, "but Elisha, the prophet who is in Israel, tells the king of Israel the very words you speak in your bedroom." "Go, find out where he is," the king ordered, "so I can send men and capture him." The report came back, "He is in Dothan." Then he sent horses and chariots and a strong force there. They went by night and surrounded the city. When the servant of the man of God got up and went out early the next morning, an army with horses and chariots had surrounded the city. "Oh my lord, what shall we do?" the servant asked. "Don't be afraid," the prophet answered. "Those who are with us are more than those who are with them."* **And Elisha prayed, "O LORD, open his eyes so he may see."** *Then the LORD opened the servant's eyes, and he looked and saw the hills full of horses and chariots of fire all around Elisha* (2 Kings 6:11-17 NIV).

One day while I was meditating on this passage, the Lord spoke to my heart and asked me a question: "Who prayed for the servant that his eyes would be opened to see?"

I said, "Lord, it was Elisha who asked You to open the servant's eyes."

The Lord then said, "Yes, but who prayed for Elisha that his eyes be opened to see?"

I said, "Lord, no one that I know of."

The Lord then said, "You are correct. No one needed to pray for Elisha to see, he lived in this realm on a consistent basis. This realm is known as the *slipstream of Heaven.*"

I then asked the Lord, "What is the slipstream of Heaven?"

The Lord responded, *"It is a heavenly flow that you can merge into where the realm of the prophet and seer anointing becomes activated in your life. In this place the deeper mysteries of My Word are revealed to you. In the slipstream, your spiritual eyesight becomes greatly illumined, and you move with much greater ease in your walk with Me. I desire for all of My people to live in this heavenly stream."*

The Lord Jesus has graciously made the slipstream of Heaven available for all of His people to access. Just as there is a heavenly slipstream, there are natural streams in the earth that point to the significance of what exists as a much greater heavenly reality.

One naturally occurring phenomenon in the earth that closely resembles the heavenly slipstream is the *jet stream.* The jet stream is one of the most powerful forces of nature. It was discovered during World War II when aviators first tried to cross the Pacific Ocean. The *jet stream* is a strong current of wind that blows faster than 200 miles per hour. It is found at altitudes of 10-15 miles, near the top of the Earth's troposphere where most of the Earth's weather takes place. During winter months, the core of the jet stream can reach speeds of 310 miles per hour.

While the jet stream can stretch for thousands of miles, it is usually only a few hundred miles wide and less than three miles thick. Jet streams encircle the earth in meandering paths, shifting positions, as well as speed, with the seasons.

Long-haul commercial airliners try to travel *with* the jet stream because of the increase in fuel efficiency, while record-attempting balloonists rely on finding and merging into powerful jet streams to cover as much distance as quickly as possible.

The first non-stop, around-the-world balloon flight occurred in March 1999, when Bertrand Piccard and Brian Jones caught the jet stream while high over North Africa. These men piloted the specially prepared balloon, the Breitling Oriber 3, into new distance, endurance, and time records, traveling around the world non-stop in 19 days, 21 hours, and 55 minutes. Catching the jet stream was crucial to their success.

Catching the heavenly slipstream can be crucial to our success as well.

Just as streams in the sky aid in speeding one along to their destination, likewise are there streams and currents in the seas that provide help to mariners. One of the most well-known ocean currents is called the *Gulf Stream*. The Gulf Stream is a warm ocean current of water in the North Atlantic ocean that flows from the Gulf of Mexico, along the northeast United States coast, and from there to the British Isles. It was first noticed in 1530 by Ponce de Leon, and the Gulf Stream was often viewed by early sailors as being a river that runs in the ocean.

Benjamin Franklin recognized the Gulf Stream as a powerful stream of water that could be used to assist the ships that delivered mail and other goods from Europe to America. Flows in the Gulf Stream have been clocked at 5 miles per hour, which can allow water in the stream to move more than 100 miles in a day.

Along with the ships and sailboats that use the current to their benefit, there are also giant sea turtles, whales, and many other sea creatures that regularly swim in the Gulf Stream. This current, along with other currents and streams that God has so wisely established in the earth, are natural indicators of heavenly realities that God desires for us to understand and make good use of.

By understanding God's natural creation we can more easily merge into the heavenly stream that can carry us faster and farther than our own human efforts. Slipping into the stream can appear to be somewhat of a puzzle at first, but when examined more closely we notice that what may seem improbable is possible when we have the necessary knowledge.

READY, SET, GO

When I was younger, I used to be in awe of people who had accomplished great athletic feats. All throughout high school and college, I competed in track, running the mile and other middle-distance races. When I was in the tenth grade, I remember checking the Sunday paper for the local and regional track meet results that were held the previous day in my home state of Texas.

The day before I had competed in a track meet and finished second place in the mile run. I felt pretty good about my time until I saw how fast some guy in San Antonio had run the mile. When I saw his time, I couldn't believe it. I actually tore that section out of the newspaper and took it to my track coach on Monday. When I showed it to him, he said, "Hmm, that must be a misprint." But it wasn't a misprint. This fellow down in South Texas was almost running a sub-four minute mile, while still in high school. To me, as a tenth grader, that level seemed completely unattainable.

However, some things that seem impossible can be attained if the right approach is taken. Later, while running track in college, I too ran a pretty good mile, 4:14 to be exact, while in my sophomore year. Not the world record, of course, but not too shabby either. I found out the only difference between me and the wonder kid down in South Texas was that he started training at a much younger age than I did. Because he started years sooner, he was able to do collegiate level workouts after just finishing the eighth grade in junior high! If I had started earlier and had professional coaching like he had, then it would have been possible for me, or any potentially talented distance runner, to have produced the same results. Insight available through these analogies will aid you in merging into the slipstream of Heaven.

When I graduated from high school, I was the district champion and runner-up in the two mile. I did the best I could with what was available to me through coaching and support, but I never got to a place where I dominated the competition. However, things were different for my younger brother. He started running at the same time I did and was two years younger than me. He also trained under a new coach who came to the school—a former top runner who was current with the best training methods.

My brother's high school track career flourished under this coach. While I was in college, I decided to drive home to watch my brother run in a high school, cross-country meet. By this time he was a senior, and the meet he was competing in was a large one with about 300 runners. The race was a three mile out and back course that was run on the beach, at

South Padre Island National Seashore. When I arrived, the race had already started, and I could see that the runners were spreading out, with a lead pack up front that had pulled ahead of everyone else—it concerned me because I did not see my brother in the lead pack.

I found his coach, and I asked him where my brother was in the race, because I didn't see him. The coach smiled and said, "Look over there." He pointed way down to the halfway marker, and there I saw my brother. My brother had already gone around the halfway point and made the turn for home toward the finish line. He was so far ahead of everyone else, that the runner in second place must have been 300 yards behind him.

Now the tables were turned. Most of those runners were probably thinking, "I could never run as fast as that guy who is up front, that's impossible." The reality is, if a person wants to run on that level, it takes a certain amount of commitment. What does it take to be a successful high school distance runner? It takes running a minimum of 80 miles a week, or 12 miles a day, which demonstrates a lot of commitment for someone who is barely old enough to drive a car. An inspiring young high school runner may ask, "What if I only want to run 20 miles a week, will that enable me to be a champion runner?" The answer is simply, "No." That low level of training won't separate you from the other runners; you'll be left far back in the pack with all the others.

Being successful requires building one's stamina and aerobic threshold to a level where running 80 miles a week is done consistently throughout the year. It's not a seasonal sport; it requires year-round training. This is what it takes to merge into the championship flow of a top caliber, high school distance runner. Are you ready to gear up and merge into the slipstream of Heaven?

Another interesting comparison with merging into an area that takes discipline to succeed in is strength training, or, sometimes known as bodybuilding. Now, up front, I want to emphasize that I'm not endorsing vanity, or suggesting that godly men and women wear revealing clothes to show off their rippling pectoral muscles and deep bronze tans.

Several years ago, I followed the online training journal of an amateur bodybuilder. This Website was professional—no pictures of women, and no profanity. It was simply about a man in his early twenties who was committed to attaining pro status as a bodybuilder. He had some previous weight training experience, but decided to chronicle his daily work-outs through an on-line journal with photos, while including all aspects of nutrition and exercise routines that were performed daily. When he started his journal, he came under the guidance and teaching of a professional bodybuilding coach.

What's amazing is that within only two years of following this system, he earned his pro card and was accepted into the pro ranks. He accomplished his goal without the use of any steroids or other banned substances. That in itself is quite a remarkable feat, when you consider how many bodybuilders are using illegal drugs to enhance their performance. The point I'm making is that it is possible to reach your goal if you are willing to make the same sacrifices that this guy was willing to make.

First of all, he was consuming 600 grams of protein per day. One cheeseburger is only about 25 grams of protein, leaving 575 grams of protein to take down. He eats ten meals a day, one meal every two hours. Only once a week he eats a dessert, and his meals are low in fat—all calories must be accounted for. Protein shakes and creatine supplements must be consumed every two hours, which also includes waking up at 3 o'clock in the morning to drink them. (This guy must make frequent trips to the bathroom!)

Then, there is the daily commitment of going to the gym early in the morning for a grueling workout. Often there are injuries, soreness, and pain. Yet this guy was willing to structure his whole life around his goal of becoming a professional bodybuilder, choosing to build a Herculean physique, instead of living a "normal," sedentary life. Some may think he looks so fit because he's genetically gifted, and the average guy can't achieve that look. Others who are informed know exactly how his physique was developed—commitment.

We need to demystify what it takes to merge into the slipstream of Heaven. Some believers think that visions, heavenly encounters, and regular supernatural experiences are only for a few select ministers who have somehow been granted a divine privilege. That is simply not true. *It takes commitment.*

QUALITY TIME

Years back, I remember reading the Book of Ezekiel, and about how Ezekiel saw into Heaven and beheld the four living creatures and other heavenly wonders. While reading through the Scripture passages, the thought dawned on me, *This guy is no different than me. He gets dressed just like me, eats food like me, has to go to the bathroom like I do. If supernatural visions and glimpses into Heaven can happen to Ezekiel, then why can't they happen to me?*

Over a period of time, I discovered that God desires for all of His people to experience the supernatural realm. I'm not talking about trying to force something or trying to make God perform a miracle just to prove a point. That kind of thinking is wrong. God can't be forced to do anything, and the Holy Spirit is the One who chooses when, where, and how to manifest the power of God. However, the encouraging thing to know is that if you hang out a lot with God in prayer and spend time meditating upon His word, you will realize how willing the Lord is to reveal an "open Heaven." The problem hasn't been God's willingness, but rather His people's lack of interest to hang out long enough with Him to see His glory.

You read about what it requires to be a champion, high school distance runner, and what is involved in the daily life of a champion bodybuilder. In a similar way, there is a level of commitment required for a person to merge into the slipstream of Heaven. In my personal life, I have discovered what frame of devotional time is necessary for me to flow in this heavenly stream.

Recently, I read in a nature article that mature eagles spend a certain amount of quality time each day in flight. I believe there is a parallel between the adult eagle's flight time and the devotional time of a spiritually mature Christian who soars in Christ. This same principle is why Elisha did not need anybody to lay hands on him and pray for the Lord to open his spiritual eyesight. He was already seeing consistently into the realm of the Spirit because his life was devoted to the Lord in prayer and meditation upon His Word.

For someone who is called into the ministry office of the prophet, there is a God-given grace, a supernatural equipping, that creates a craving for solitude. While not all are called into the ministry office of a prophet, everyone can experience the slipstream of Heaven by spending quality time with God. Of course, there are some who say that it is impossible for the average person to spend much time with the Lord every day in prayer and still fulfill their responsibilities in life. While it is true that the Lord supplies a divine grace for a fulltime minister to have this amount of time available, my first question, however, to those who would think they cannot find available quality time for the Lord is, "How much time do you spend watching television each day?"

Statistics show that the average American watches from six to eight hours of television *every day*. Considering that most polls show very little difference between Christians and non-Christians—whether divorce statistics, health-related surveys, or evaluations conducted on time spent watching television—I would have to conclude that cutting back on television would be the first place to redeem time that can be better spent with the Lord.

Entering the slipstream of Heaven is not a cakewalk. It takes discipline, commitment, determination, and intense spiritual hunger to enter a place with God where He knows that He can whisper His secrets into your heart, and commune with you in a realm where things that are sacred and holy are held in highest regard. A person has to be willing to structure their life around such a passion, while still fulfilling their daily responsibilities and duties.

The Lord gave me another Scripture reference, along with the previous passage from Second Kings 6:17, to demonstrate the reality of the slipstream of Heaven. The second reference is found in the Book of Isaiah, and it provides a great motivation to rise up and enter this place of boundless joy and peace.

> *And a highway will be there; it will be called the Way of Holiness. The unclean will not journey on it; it will be for those who walk in that Way, wicked fools will not go about on it. No lion will be there, nor will any ferocious beast get up on it; they will not be found there. But only the redeemed will walk there, and the ransomed of the LORD will return. They will enter Zion with singing; everlasting joy will crown their heads. Gladness and joy will overtake them, and sorrow and sighing will flee away* (Isaiah 35:8-10 NIV).

The word *highway* in the Hebrew language refers to "a raised path." The reference is regarding an easy and uninterrupted return of the Jews from captivity to their homeland, while at the same time signifying a path to Heaven that is available to believer's to walk on who are pure in heart. Not only will unclean sinners not be allowed on this path, but neither would unclean persons be permitted to walk on this holy road. It is a path of separation from the world.

Only the purified Church has access to this raised path, a path that has been so elevated that no lion or wild beast can jump high enough to reach it. The only ones encountered on this path are the pilgrims who are heading toward their eternal home in God. These are the ones whom God has delivered and set free from bondage and the enemy's affliction. While it doesn't mean that satan can't cause problems for those who walk this path, it does make us secure in knowing that as we walk the King's Highway, no real harm can come to us. We have divine security, and the wicked one cannot touch us.

There is a key verse in the New Testament that brings much insight into entering the slipstream of Heaven.

> *In those days when the number of disciples was increasing, the Grecian Jews among them complained against the Hebraic Jews because their widows were being overlooked in the daily distribution of food. So the Twelve gathered all the disciples together and said, "It would not be right for us to neglect the ministry of the word of God in order to wait on tables. Brothers, choose seven men from among you who are known to be full of the Spirit and wisdom. We will turn this responsibility over to them and we will give our attention to prayer and the ministry of the word* (Acts 6:1-4 NIV).

The twelve apostles had a method of operation that their ministries were based upon. The early apostles centered their lives on much time in prayer and then ministering the Word of God. They were very smart to not allow themselves to be distracted by side issues that would have caused them to deviate from their primary focus.

Today, I see many ministers who are majoring on minors. There is always a temptation for ministers to become engulfed in doing the work of the Kingdom, so much in fact that personal time with the Lord becomes a distant priority. This is why some ministries have become more like machines than ministries. A machine can operate by itself as long as it receives minimum maintenance. What's not good about this is that eventually the machine becomes a monster that has to be continually fed and ends up consuming innocent people. This is why prayer is so important, because a minister who truly spends quality time in prayer will remain humble even when great success overtakes him or her.

Today, satan has released an evil spirit who tries to influence the thought patterns of ministers by suggesting to them, "You don't need to spend all that time in prayer. That's boring. Do something more practical." But, that is a lie of the devil. I like how the New American Standard Bible translates verse 4.

> But we will **devote** ourselves to prayer and the ministry of the word (Acts 6:4 NASB).

The Lord is truly seeking those ministers today who are *devoted* to Him in prayer and the ministry of the Word. To be devoted means one is loyal and constant to what God stresses the emphasis on in His Word. This level of devotion is what it takes to run with the horses and work with angels.

While some may argue that such a view of devotion is excessive or fanatical, I choose not to debate over the subject, but rather pursue what I have discovered to be effective in my personal life and ministry. One of the easiest and most refreshing ways to merge into the slipstream of Heaven is by praying in tongues for extended periods of time. Even if a person does not have a large block of uninterrupted time available for non-stop prayer, a few minutes here or there can really become a lot in the course of an entire day.

I personally do not have a scheduled prayer time, but I pray whenever there is free time to do so. Whether morning, noon, or night, I have found that the Lord is always available to listen. Praying in tongues will greatly strengthen a believer on the *inside*. Apostle Paul said, *"He that speaks in an unknown tongue edifies himself..."* (1 Cor. 14:4). Speaking in tongues builds up and strengthens our inward being.

Jude, in his letter to the church, made the following statement: *"But you, beloved, building up yourselves on your most holy faith, praying in the Holy Ghost..."* (Jude 20). Here Jude also points out the dynamic of inward development that occurs when we pray in tongues.

The moment Spirit-filled believers open their mouths and begin to pray in tongues, they cross over into the supernatural realm. It takes time for the physical body to calm down, and it takes even longer for the mind to reach a state of peace and calmness where the "gears" in our head are no longer turning. Once a condition of peaceful neutrality for the body and mind is reached through praying in the Spirit, then our inner being is much more sensitive to the guidance of the Holy Spirit.

PRAYING IN THE SPIRIT

I first became aware of the great benefits of praying in the Spirit for extended periods of time back in the early '90s. I drove my car to see a movie at a theatre, and after it was over I walked out and found that my car would not start. I didn't have a cell phone to call for help, so I decided to walk all the way home—about ten miles. It took me about two hours. As I began my walk home, I decided to pray in tongues all the way while walking. When I got home after praying in the Spirit for two hours, I noticed my fingers were completely numb and the palms of my hands felt very hot. This was a tangible manifestation of the anointing of God's Spirit. Since then, I have enjoyed praying in tongues every day.

Back in the Old Testament, all the gifts of the Spirit were in operation except for tongues and interpretation of tongues. Speaking in tongues is exclusive for this church-age dispensation. Speaking in tongues stirs up our spirits and allows us to move into the other gifts of the Spirit more easily. In most of

my ministry meetings, the Spirit of the Lord consistently comes upon me to prophesy to individuals. Because I set aside preparation time before my meetings by praying in the Spirit, the gifts of the Spirit, especially prophecy, come forth with ease. Usually, by the time I've finished ministering, the Spirit of Prophecy has also come upon the pastor of the church, and he begins to prophesy as well.

Speaking in tongues catapults us into the greater gifts and manifestations of God's Spirit. I'm convinced the apostle Paul had a deep understanding of the great value of praying in tongues for extended periods of time, for he wrote:

> *I thank God that I speak in tongues more than all of you...* (1 Corinthians 14:18 NIV).

When Paul was traveling on those long journeys by ship and walking long distances by foot, I'm sure he had a lot of time to pray in the Spirit as he went along. Praying in the Spirit has an energizing and illuminating effect upon our inner being. I always enjoy our ministry travels because driving from state to state or across the country allows me to drive for many hours, providing lots of extra time to speak in tongues as I go. While driving down the highway and praying in the Spirit, I often sense the certainty that even though I'm traveling on a paved highway, I have also merged onto the highway of holiness, and I'm moving in the slipstream of Heaven.

Chapter Six

HORSES AND ANGELS

HORSES AND ANGELS

When the Lord first spoke to me about writing a book about angels, He, at the same time, impressed upon my heart that it would also spiritually relate to horses. For over a year, I was puzzled about how to even start writing a book about angels that would in some way also refer to horses. I thought to myself, *This sure is an odd mix, angels and horses; I wonder what the Lord is up to!* Several times I tried to start writing the book, but had no anointing to write, probably because I didn't know the direction that the Lord had for the book.

When the Lord directed my wife and I to move from out West to Moravian Falls, North Carolina in 2005, we obeyed. We did not know anyone when we first arrived, but the Lord quickly introduced us to wonderful people who welcomed us and encouraged us in our ministry. One day, a new friend

invited me to lunch and said he wanted to introduce me to a local land developer who was developing a subdivision close by. When we got to lunch, I met the businessman. For the first ten or fifteen minutes, our conversation centered on normal, everyday talk.

Then the subject came up about me writing a second book and that the topic was angels. The businessman's eyes lit up, and he said, "Did you know that there are a lot of similarities between horses and angels?" When he made that statement he immediately caught my attention. He owns several horses and has been a horse lover for many years. During that lunch conversation, I knew that the Lord brought us together and was revealing a clearer understanding of how to work in harmony with the angels through understanding natural examples about how horses are known to behave.

I will share with you some "cues" (a horse training word) that shed light on the relevance between the way horses behave and the way angels respond. These cues come from my discussions with this new friend, and I am thankful to him for sharing his insights about horses with me. It's now time for God's people to walk with God, run with the horses, and work with the angels.

OPEN THE GATES

One of the most notable traits about horses is that they will gravitate toward an open gate. If there are ten horses standing on the backside of a pasture, and there is an open gate on the far side of the field, the horses will begin moving toward the open gate. As to why they do this, I can't exactly say. Perhaps it's because the horse senses an increase in freedom and continually seeks a greater place of openness.

P5. 24 [handwritten]

Like horses, angels also move toward open gates. Gates can also be referred to as portals. There is such a thing as a heavenly portal. I believe there are heavenly portals—specific places on earth where the veil separating the spirit realm from the natural realm is very thin. In the area where I live, there are several mountains along with several rock formations where consistent angelic and heavenly manifestations occur. These are places where either much prayer has occurred over a long period of time, or it just happens to be where the Lord has chosen to place a spiritual landmark, much like Jacob discovered Bethel to be when he encountered the Lord while sleeping with his head resting on a stone one night. It was in Bethel where Jacob saw a stairway reaching from earth to Heaven with the angels of God going up and down on it. (see Gen. 28:11-13). I'm sure that Jacob had spent the night in many different places, but it wasn't until he was in Bethel that he saw such a glorious vision.

P5.24: We Are His Gates which He Comes Through. [handwritten]

There are other "Bethel's" in the earth today that God has established as portals or stairways of heavenly activity. Of course, if a person does not spend time with God regularly in prayer, it is difficult to recognize these portals, and almost impossible to take advantage of them. Jacob encountered the Lord at Bethel, although at first he wasn't aware of how special the place was until he had spent the night there.

> *Then Jacob awoke from his sleep and said, "Surely the Lord is in this place, and I wasn't even aware of it"* (Genesis 28:16 NLT).

Being aware of gates and heavenly portals can help us cooperate with the plan of Heaven. Most of the writing I do occurs while I am in Moravian Falls, North Carolina. There is simply an anointing to write in this area, and there is a noted

mountain in Moravian Falls that is confirmed by many to be walked by scribe angels. It is the scribe angels who are involved with helping God's people write books that God desires to be written and published in the earth. The original manuscripts are in Heaven and the scribe angels help transfer those messages from Heaven to earth through heavenly thoughts and inspiration.

It was in February 2005 when the Lord spoke to my wife through a dream and instructed us to move to Moravian Falls. Although we had no ministry contacts in the East and had never ministered east of the Mississippi River, my wife and I both had a great peace and inward witness that it was the perfect will of God for us to move from Nevada all the way across the country to North Carolina.

The day after we had committed to move, we noticed that the house across from our home that we were renting had sold. The house had been on the market for almost three months before it sold. Within a few days a large moving truck arrived and was unloaded with everything for the new family. When my wife and I introduced ourselves, they said they were from, "North Carolina." When we told them we would be moving there in a few weeks, the wife said, "Why don't you take and use all of our new moving boxes and wardrobe boxes for your trip." We gratefully accepted the kind offer and used their boxes to move our belongings back across the country. Just days before we left, the Lord also provided us with the thousands of dollars we needed for the trip. He provided many other amazing confirmations as well to help boost our faith and trust in Him.

OPEN PORTALS

Once we arrived in Moravian Falls, my wife and I could tell there was an unusual anointing over specific areas. There is a heavenly canopy that exists over certain areas that is so strong that my wife and I can tell where it begins and ends when we drive around in our car. I believe that the two reasons the Lord brought my family to this place is for me to pray and write—two of my favorite things to do.

History indicates that the Moravian missionaries from Germany committed this land to the Lord through a prayer of dedication, and that the true deed to the land belongs to the Lord. Some historians have also said that Moravian Falls was the publishing capital of America during the mid 1800s. The anointing for prayer and writing is quite evident here.

Just as horses are attracted to open gates, angels also travel through portals to and from Heaven with information that we need to receive. Jacob understood the importance of his "Bethel." Don't close the gate of your heart to the ministry of the angels just because some people might think you are "too far out there." Some Christians are too content where they are when it comes to spirituality in the Lord. I don't mind being "way out there," as long as I'm "way out there" on the Word.

Many years back while living in Lubbock, Texas, I remember talking to a man about an apartment he had for rent. While talking to him we somehow got onto the subject of faith in God, and I shared with him that I was a Christian. He told me that he was a Christian too, and we began discussing some Bible topics. However, the conversation began to deteriorate when he brought up strange topics and voiced his strong opinions. I finally had to stop him and say, "Where is this stuff that you are talking about found in the Bible? I've never read it before." He said, "Oh, it's not in there. I'm way beyond that!"

Well, I didn't rent the apartment. I decided I didn't want to be living next door to a so-called Christian who had no respect for the integrity of the Bible. We do not need to be afraid of the ministry of the angels because their ministry is clearly based upon the Word of God.

BONDING WITH THOSE THEY KNOW

(intersecting)

Another interesting similarity between horses and angels is that they will only bond with those they know. A horse will only bond with someone it trusts. Over the last 20 years, there have been many breakthroughs in methods of training and working with horses. While these proper methods have been around for a long time, it has only been in the last 20 years that they have become widely accepted in equestrian society.

The old method of breaking a horse through forced submission and intimidation has proven to be detrimental in the long-term relationship between horse and owner. It is not necessary to break a horse and crush his spirit in order for him to be taught basic skills, such as carrying a rider or overcoming the fear of entering a trailer. In the old days horses were beaten, whipped, or starved into submission in an effort to get a horse to perform a certain task.

Unfortunately, many of these same violent practices continue today by horse owners who are deficient in correct horse-training knowledge. These harmful and degrading methods quench the horse's inward fire, thus shutting down ingrained God-given natural attributes. A horse may bow to intimidation and fear tactics, but it will never respect the one forcing it to do so.

When a horse bonds with its owner, there is mutual respect and cooperation. Bonding requires patience because it takes time and is an ongoing process. Bonding requires spending quality time together, especially in a non-working environment where demands are not made. The best way to bond with a horse is to simply hang out together and have fun getting to know each other.

A horse will bond with its owner when they can sense unconditional love. Horses (and people) love to be spoken to gently and treated with affection. They especially find pleasure in being stroked and rubbed, and being kept well cleaned and brushed. A horse's feet should be checked and cleaned out daily. Their shoes need to be inspected as well. Horses love to be washed with warm water after a good exercise and before being turned into the stall. They need plenty of fresh water and hay every day.

Massaging a horse around the eyes and between the ears brings peaceful comfort. Gently cleaning out their nostrils with a soft, wet cloth removes dirt and gunk, while relieving irritation caused by biting flies and gnats. It's also good to wipe around their mouth and eyes and even rub therapeutic aroma oils on their coat. This produces an exceptionally tranquil state for the horse to relax in as he is being groomed. It's good to feel around the entire body of the horse, checking for muscle tightness or any abnormalities. If bug bites are discovered then it is good to rub the spot with hydrogen peroxide, which disinfects the area and proves to be especially refreshing for the horse.

These consistent acts of kindness will cause a horse to desire you above other people. The horse will come to you when you call or when it sees you, and the person who understands how to make a horse contented will be rewarded with a cherished relationship.

My daughter and I have a great relationship that runs very deep because I spend time with her simply because I like being with her. I'm not trying to get her to do something for me; we just enjoy having fun together. If I only spent time with her in order to make sure her homework was correctly done then a bonding relationship would not develop.

Many Christians have a difficult time bonding with the Holy Scriptures that admonish them to come up to a higher place in God, but they seem to have no problem bonding to the television or to treasured hobbies. However, a wonderful relationship with God opens the door to many exciting realities within the Kingdom of Light. As we walk near to God, we can expect to gain awareness and appreciation of our friends, the angels. We see in the Scriptures that many ministers in the Bible developed a relationship and were familiar with the angel that God had assigned to help them. God said to Moses:

> *"See, I am sending **an angel** before you to protect you on your journey and lead you safely to the place I have prepared for you. **Pay close attention to him, and obey his instructions**. Do not rebel against him, for he is my representative, and he will not forgive your rebellion. But if you are careful to obey him, following all my instructions, then I will be an enemy to your enemies, and I will oppose those who oppose you. For **my angel will go before you and bring you into the land** of the Amorites, Hittites,*

*Perizzites, Canaanites, Hivites, and Jebusites, so you may
live there. And I will destroy them completely"* (Exodus
23:20-23 NIV).

Sometimes theologians say the angels that appeared so
many times in the Old Testament were actually theophanies
of the Lord, who appeared in different forms because He had
not yet received His physical body as He later received it
when He walked the earth for 33 $1/_2$ years. The word *theophany* is a term describing the physical manifestation of God
that is displayed particularly through an individual. This
thought about the angels being theophanies of the Lord is
taken because often when the angels speak they say, "Thus
saith the Lord..." This makes it appear that it was not an
angel, but rather God speaking.

However, angels sent by God are authorized to speak on
behalf of the Lord. Often in the Bible there are angels
speaking in the *first person* form, much like a prophet does
when he is under a strong anointing and is completely
yielded to God. A prophet under the anointing may say,
"Thus saith the Lord..." but that doesn't mean that the
prophet is actually a theophany. It just means that he or she
is a vessel through whom the Lord can speak.

For instance, in a meeting several years ago the Spirit of
Prophecy came upon the minister hosting the meeting, and
he said, "*I* tried to give the laptop computer industry to a
Spirit-filled believer, but he refused to obey *Me*, so *I* had to
take it to someone in the world instead." Through this
example, do you see how the Spirit of God was speaking
through this minister in the first person sense? Angels often
deliver messages in the same format. There are certainly
theophanies that occurred in the Bible, such as the time

Abraham was visited by the three men. One of the men was without doubt the Lord, but the angel visits in the Bible are not all theophanies. Most of the cases were those of angels sent by God with a message.

The person who has a close relationship with his or her angel is in a position to make greater strides with God. The minister who has learned to value the angelic help that God has assigned is positioned to receive information from God with a clear message for the present time. Zechariah was a person who experienced supernatural insight through an angelic messenger.

> **So the angel that communed with me** *said unto me, Cry thou, saying, Thus saith the LORD of hosts; I am jealous for Jerusalem and Zion with a great jealousy* (Zechariah 1:14).

The phrase *the angel that communed with me* implies more than just a little chat, but rather an extended conversation that took place between the prophet Zechariah and the angel. Of course, any message from an angel must be in line with the Word of God, especially the New Testament. All spirits must be judged by the Word of God in order to know if the message is true or false.

> *Beloved, do not believe every spirit, but test the spirits, whether they are of God; because many false prophets have gone out into the world* (1 John 4:1 NKJV).

Just because there are false prophets and deceptive spirits doesn't mean we just shut the whole thing down. There are false prophecies, but we should still prophesy. There is counterfeit money, but I still use cash on a regular basis. That's why it's so important that we develop an in-depth knowledge of God's Word so we can discern the genuine from the false.

MY PERSONAL ANGEL

Having a wonderful relationship with the Lord has produced the surplus benefit of allowing me to develop a close bond with my personal angel. There have been quite a few occasions when I have been awakened early in the morning by my ministry angel, who has grabbed my hand and helped pull me up from the bed, while saying, "Get up, it's time to pray." In my own natural strength, I don't think I could have done it most of those times because I was very tired. But God is releasing His great grace in these last days and is sending His angels like never before to help us as we draw near to Him. Moses became very familiar with the angel who was assigned to help him. Elijah also listened to the advice that his angel gave him.

> *The angel of the LORD said to Elijah, "Go down with him; do not be afraid of him." So Elijah got up and went down with him to the king* (2 Kings 1:15 NIV).

Becoming familiar with the angel God has assigned to you requires spending much time with the Lord and leaning into the biblical reality that *you do have a guardian angel*, as well as other potential angels who may be assigned to you.

> *See that you do not look down on one of these little ones. For I tell you that their angels in heaven always see the face of my Father in heaven* (Matthew 18:10 NIV).

I enjoyed reading about the time when Brother Kenneth Hagin had a visitation from the Lord. When the Lord appeared to him, there was an angel who stood next to the Lord. Brother Hagin asked the Lord who the angel was, and the Lord said, "He is your angel. You don't lose your angel just because you grow up." Our guardian angels are with us

all the time and more angels may be assigned to us from the Lord as we grow and develop in our walk with Him. The more sensitive we become to the Holy Spirit, the more clearly we can work with our angels.

Many Christians have a difficult time picking up on heavenly realities because they have allowed their spiritual senses to be dulled by worldly pollution. When I say pollution, I'm not referring to smog or toxic waste, but to elements that clog up a person's ability to discern spiritual truth. Many of God's own people choose to fill their minds with horror movies, graphic violence, and rude and crude forms of polluted media. This type of input keeps a person from properly discerning the leading of the Holy Spirit. Worldly pollution muddies the spiritual waters of the soul.

One of the primary attributes of the Holy Spirit is that He is holy. If a child of God allows his human spirit to become calloused and dull through the input of unholy sights and sounds, then the pipeline from the Holy Spirit to the heart of the believer gets clogged with filth.

Before I entered the ministry fulltime, I worked in the plumbing industry. I've had the distinct and humbling privilege of unclogging many sewer and drain lines. It's a nasty job, and I believe all plumbers should earn a good income because it's hard and dirty work. There were times when I had to crawl underneath old junky mobile homes and lay on my back in raw sewage while I repaired broken and leaking cast iron sewer pipes. Plumbing is not a glamorous job, but it certainly is an honorable profession.

Many of God's saints need to live up to the title of "saint" and raise their level of morality and integrity to a biblical standard. No more dirty, unclean living, but rather strive for holiness and purity of heart. Sin grieves the Holy Spirit and hinders the flow of revelation from Heaven. There must be a pure pipeline in order for the oil of the Holy Spirit to flow into the heart of the believer. If the pipeline is clogged with filth, then the oil will not flow.

I remember when I could not make it to a plumbing assignment one day because I had a ministry luncheon that I needed to attend. I called and said I couldn't come in, and the Lord always blessed me with much favor to take off for ministry engagements. When I came back to work the following day, I found out that the Lord had really blessed me. I worked with my father in-law who had been a Master Plumber for 34 years. He told me that the day I missed they were called to snake out the drain lines at the liposuction clinic. He explained how he went through five pairs of thick leather gloves snaking out all of the blubber and fat that had clogged up the lines.

While there is a problem in America with heart disease, caused by people eating fat- loaded foods which clog their arteries, we should be more concerned about not clogging up our *spiritual* arteries which carry the nourishment of Heaven into our eternal spirits. Spiritual sensitivity requires shutting off all forms of pollution that grieves the Holy Spirit. This is a sacrifice that many Christians are not willing to make, but for those who do, the rewards are tremendous. Having good spiritual health affects every area of our lives, and makes everything we do in life more colorful and vibrant.

Having a clear conduit and knowing your personal angel can become more of a reality when you respect the Lord regarding the angel which He has assigned to you. Some of the

Native American Indians took great care of their horses and spent much time with them to form an inseparable bond between man and horse. Very few cultures have ever taken the bonding process between man and horse as far as the Plains Indians did. Some Plains Indian braves actually slept with their horses at night when out on long hunting trips or on raiding parties. The brave would sleep with his face right next to the horse's mouth so that the horse could learn his owner's breath. This allowed the horse to find his owner should they be separated, even in pitch dark with no moonlight, and with other people around.

Just as horses will only bond with those they know, so will angels only work in harmony to the greatest extent with those who respect their presence and with those who are sensitive to the Holy Spirit.

Several years ago, I was in a place of transition when I was working a 40-hour week secular job while also ministering often on the weekends. This is a difficult place for ministers to pass through because you are burning the candle on both ends. It requires a careful balance of performing secular work and ministry, while trying to be a good husband, father, and maintaining a fruitful prayer life all at the same time.

I believe the Lord allows this place of transition to be very tough on purpose for those who are called into the full-time ministry. The difficulties produce a process that thins out the ranks, thus separating those who are totally sold out to the call from those who are not committed to going all the way. It was during this time when I found myself in a place of weakness just moments before I was to minister in a midweek church service. Monday and Tuesday were long- hour work days for me, but I was able to take Wednesday off to prepare for the evening service. Although I had the day off and spent much of it in prayer, I was still fatigued from not having enough sleep. But I would much rather go into a meeting tired and prayed up, then go in fully rested but not having spent preparation in prayer.

By the time the meeting rolled around, I felt ready in my spirit, but pretty lethargic in my body. After having completed the praise and worship time, the pastor of the church leaned over to me and said he was going to introduce me to speak after the offering was received. I looked back over my shoulder and saw about 300 spiritually hungry people sitting in the audience expecting a good meeting. I said to the Lord, "O Lord, you have to help me, I'm so tired tonight and I feel so weak. Please help me."

As soon as I had whispered that to the Lord, the offering time was completed, and the pastor jumped up and said, "Why don't we sing one more song before we bring Brother Steven up. Let's all stand." As we stood up, I determined in my heart to give God a sacrifice of praise. I sure didn't feel like praising the Lord, but I made the effort to bless the Lord despite being very tired. As the song progressed, I sang from my heart and lifted my right hand up high to bless the Lord. When I did that, someone on my left side grabbed my left hand that was hanging down and lifted it up high over my head.

When I looked to my left to see who raised my hand, my spiritual eyes were opened and I saw my angel standing there next to me, and he had a big smile on his face while he continued singing along with all of us. He had both of his hands raised up high and was singing while holding my left hand in his up raised right hand. Instantly, a supernatural energy went through my body and all fatigue left me. As soon as the song

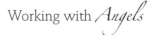

ended, the pastor said, "Brother Steven, come on up!" Well, when I walked up to the platform to minister, I walked up in the power of the Spirit of God. We had a great meeting that night. The Word of God was preached, the Holy Spirit moved, and people were commenting on how I was such a "lively" preacher who had so much energy.

Allow the Holy Spirit to help you become comfortable and familiar with the precious angel that God has assigned to you.

THE SOFT SPOT

The Bible has much to say about the tender mercies of God. King David spoke of this in the Psalms as he wrote by the inspiration of the Holy Spirit.

The LORD is good to all: and his tender mercies are over all his works (Psalm 145:9).

The fuller Hebrew meaning of this verse describes God's tender mercies as hovering above and surrounding all of His creatures. The tender mercies of God can be described as loving, affectionate, caring, adorable, precious, and sweet. The apostle Paul also wrote of God's tender mercies as he described the way he felt for the Christians in Philippi.

For God is my witness, how I long after you all in the tender mercies of Christ Jesus (Philippians 1:8 ASV).

There is a very precious and divine substance that flows from the loving reaches of God's pure heart that is called *tender mercies*. We see the tender mercies of God revealed in the illustration of the horse in what is known as the *soft spot*. The soft spot on a horse is a special place known as the *withers*, which is located just above the saddle notch, where the saddle rests on the upper shoulders of a horse. This is the place of affection where a mother horse caresses her young foal or colt. The mother horse may lick her baby horse on this special spot with her tongue, or nudge the young horse with her nose in a playful way. This conveys love and assurance to the new-born horse. Sometimes the mother horse may knick or gently kick the young horse to express displeasure with the youngster's misconduct.

The soft spot that all horses have allows tenderness to be given and received. Over the years, I have come to realize that angels also have a soft spot that allows them to be capable of being touched with the tender mercies of God. Prophet William Branham would often sing a particular song in his tent meetings that he said his ministry angel loved. When the song was sung, the angel would come, and then Brother Branham would operate in a remarkable prophetic gift accompanied by miracles of divine healing and signs and wonders. The song that his personal angel loved was, "Only Believe."

> Only believe, only believe,
> All things are possible, only believe,
> Only believe, only believe,
> All things are possible, only believe.

(Written by Paul Rader - 1921)

This may seem a little strange to some people that angels can be touched like this, but I have seen many people touched in services when a certain song was sung by an anointed singer. I've ministered in Baptist churches, and when someone sings a song about the Lord's return, it often seems like there's not a dry eye in the building. While I also am looking for and expecting the Lord's return, I don't usually break out into tears when I hear songs about His reappearance.

We are all unique, what may touch one person deeply may not have the same effect on another. However, we all have a soft spot, a place of tenderness where we are susceptible to the Holy Spirit's sweet touch. Whether it's playing Christian music in your home, reading your Bible out loud, or singing praises to God, there's something special that you do that as you walk with the Lord catches your angel's attention. Take time to notice and be sensitive to the *soft spot* that God created in your angel.

WORKING PRIMARILY BY CUES

Highly trained and experienced horses work primarily by cues, and not by voice commands. For instance, a well-trained horse understands that when you lay the neck rein on the right side of his neck, that is a cue for him to turn left. Squeezing your legs together against an experienced horse is a cue for the horse to go faster. If an inexperienced rider gets on a well- trained horse, and the rider becomes afraid because he is uncomfortable with the horse's speed, the rider may squeeze his legs together in an effort to hold on tighter. This is a mistake, because the horse thinks the rider wants him to go faster, so the horse obeys. Miscues can send the wrong signal to a horse.

Husbands and wives who have been married for a long time can sometimes understand each other just by seeing certain facial expressions, regardless of whether any words are spoken. While we certainly know that angels aren't horses, there is something about angels that enables them to pick up on our cues, whether we realize that we are sending cues or not.

A good way to demonstrate this is by the way horses trained for English riding interact with their riders when jumping over obstacles on a competitive course. When a horse approaches a fence (technically called a gate) to jump over it, the horse may balk (come to a sudden stop) if the rider is looking down. Perhaps you've seen this on television shows. I've seen horses stop so abruptly just before jumping a fence that the rider is thrown forward over the horse's head, causing the rider a long and rough fall to the ground. Proper riding technique requires the rider to look forward toward the next jump as he is in the process of making his current jump. Horses seem to possess a sixth sense, in that they know when the rider looks down, instead of being focused ahead for the next jump.

Angels know when we are hesitant to trust God because of doubt and unbelief. They sense when we take our eyes off of the Lord; and when this takes place, they stop working on our behalf.

Recently, I was visiting with a dear friend of mine, Anna Rountree, who is a precious woman of God. Anna wrote the book, *The Heavens Opened* which details her experience of being caught up to Heaven and the messages she received from God the Father that He desired for her to bring back to earth and share with His people. While speaking with Anna, I asked her to explain to me how the visions began and what took place when she first went to Heaven. She described how, in a vision, she saw an angel appear just a few feet in front of her as she was sitting in a chair in a lake cabin with her husband, Albert. As her eyes were opened to see into the realm of the Spirit, the angel spoke to her: "Come forward."

Her spiritual body rose from the chair and began to follow the angel. Two other angels opened a tall, gossamer, blue curtain to allow them to pass through. Once through this set of curtains she began to have an internal argument with herself. She had never had a visionary experience like this one, and her logical mind began to challenge her spirit.

The angel turned and held out his right hand for her to stop. "Stop," he said. She stopped in her tracks as—internally—her mind and her spirit limped between two opinions: was this or was this not from God. Once her spirit gained the victory in this internal argument, the angel knew it.

"Come forward," he reiterated, leading her through two more tall, blue curtains that were held open by angels. More and more light poured through these curtains.

When she passed through the third curtain she found herself standing before a blazing, white light on the "sea of glass" in Heaven. From there she received her commissioning from the heavenly Father to experience and record a series of divinely granted heavenly visits that were destined for her to fulfill.

The point of this story: angels can sense when we hesitate in our faith. Sending cues of doubt and hesitancy cause the angels to stop in their assistance to us, leaving us helpless until we refocus and choose to fully trust God.

Not long ago, while ministering in a church in Nevada, I prophesied to a particular Christian brother who was in his early thirties. I prophesied that he was going to have an angelic visitation. About a week later, when he was studying his Bible, he was suddenly overcome by the glory of the Lord. He fell on his knees to worship God, and he later described to me how an intense burning heat began to move through his body, causing him to perspire heavily. He said the cause for the great heat was an angel of the Lord who stood over him and allowed him to sense the love and holiness of God.

He said that as the angel stood over him, the Holy Spirit began to deal with him about certain sinful habits that he needed to lay down. After confessing his sin and committing to walk more closely with the Lord, he finally felt the heat subside. This event lasted for about two hours before he was able to get up. After the encounter he was more committed than ever to serve the Lord. When he described this experience to me, the Spirit of the Lord came upon me, and I prophesied to him, saying, "Your younger brother will have a visitation as well!"

The younger brother was 17 years of age and wasn't really serving the Lord. He came to church only to please his older brother who was his legal guardian. The younger brother was living a life displeasing to the Lord. He wanted to have fun in the world while hoping to be good enough to make it to Heaven. Two weeks after I spoke the prophetic word, the younger brother testified in a Sunday morning church service that the night before he was sitting on his bed in his bedroom. He said an angel came through the ceiling and hovered above him in the air and said, "Come with me, I want to show you Heaven."

The young brother was hesitant and replied, "I don't want to come yet." The angel made another attempt, but this time his strength to carry the young brother appeared to be lessened as the angel again said, "Come with me, I want to show you Heaven." The young brother said he told the angel, "Not now, but later." The angel made a third attempt, and it was clear that the strength of the angel was quickly fading. After a third refusal by the young brother, the angel departed by going upward through the ceiling of the room.

I wish this story had a happy ending, but the younger brother slipped into an immoral relationship that he was unwilling to forsake only a few days after sharing his testimony in church. It's amazing to me the grace that God has for humankind as He tries to throw out a lifeline to those who are sinking in sin, but yet a person has to be willing to grab that line. Doubt and unbelief are sin, and these sins along with others hinder God's holy angels from rendering the aid that they are meant to supply.

Don't send angels wrong cues by entertaining negative and sinful thoughts. We need to speak words that are filled with faith and say things that glorify God so that the angels can work in harmony with us to the fullest potential.

OTHER INTERESTING SIMILARITIES

Horses have the unusual ability to sleep while standing up. God designed the legs of a horse in a special way so they form a system of interlocking ligaments and bones, which works as a sling to suspend the weight of their body without causing strain. A horse can be completely relaxed as he sleeps standing up and does not have to exert any energy to stay balanced. Most horses do the majority of their sleeping from a standing position since it appears that lying down is uncomfortable on their internal organs and can also cause muscle cramps. Horse experts also agree that the horse sleeps standing up because it is a built-in defense mechanism which protects the horse from being vulnerable to predators and being caught by surprise.

In like comparison, angels do not have to lie down and sleep because they do not possess physical bodies like we do.

Several days ago, I had lunch with a pastor of a local church. Over lunch he shared his testimony with me about how God delivered him from a life of sin involving heavy drug usage when he was a teenager. When this pastor was a young teenage boy, he got caught up with the wrong crowd and was urged to use drugs. Although he gave his life to the Lord when he was eight years of age, he never matured spiritually because of a lack of mentoring. The church where he was saved didn't take him forward with teaching or show him how to study his Bible and pray.

His parents were divorced, and he lived alone with his father in Southern California. His father eventually became a Christian who loved God and daily prayed for his son, but the young son chose to rebel and pursue a life of sin and lawlessness. As time progressed, this young man sank deeper and deeper into the usage of many types of drugs. The downward spiral of sin greatly saddened the Christian father. One night the teenage boy came home very late and crawled into bed to go to sleep. As he pulled the covers up to his chest, he suddenly was lifted up out of his body and was carried by the Holy Spirit to another room in the house.

The Holy Spirit carried him to his father's bedroom, and there he could see his father lying in the bed asleep. To the son's surprise, he saw eight angels walking in a circle around his father's bed. Each angel had some type of musical instrument in his hand, and they were playing these instruments to soothe and calm the father as he slept. Even though there was a wall directly behind the father's bed, the angels would walk right through it as they slowly walked around the bed in a full circle. Shocked by what he was seeing, the young man tried to call out, saying, "Dad!" The moment he did that his spirit traveled immediately back to the bed where he had come from. His spirit jumped right back into his body and as soon as he did, the cry, "Dad!" popped right out of his mouth.

Through this experience and others, this young teenager eventually yielded his life to the Lord and was instantly delivered from cigarettes, drugs, and alcohol. Today, he is a pastor who has a wonderful wife and family as well as a strong and growing church with a special emphasis on reaching out to those who are considered to be the rejects of society. Although this man's father was not aware of the angels in his room as he slept, it is comforting to know that the Lord can minister to us through His angels even when we sleep. The angels do not need sleep as we do, and they can stand on guard around the clock and can be ready for action at a moment's notice.

Horses also have a remarkable sense of being able to find their way home. It's possible for a rider to just sit back in the saddle and read, write, or pray while the horse uses his built-in autopilot to head toward home. This is actually how the famous minister John Wesley wrote most of his psalms and writings and even did his Bible study. He did most of it while on horseback, thus making the best use of his time as he traveled on a ministry circuit preaching in many different places.

I don't know if that method would have worked very well for me. Usually, I experience motion sickness if I try reading while in the back seat of a car when driving through hills and turns. While history doesn't tell us exactly what kind of horse Wesley rode, it must have had a nice, smooth stride that allowed him to focus on what he was doing without being distracted. Throughout his ministry, John Wesley traveled over 250,000 miles on horseback while preaching over 40,000 sermons throughout England, Ireland, and Scotland. He usually ministered two or three times each day and did so up until the age of 86.

During his journeys on horseback he compiled an English dictionary, wrote 233 books, published 23 collections of hymns, and recorded daily preaching experiences in his journal spanning the years 1735-1790 which produced four volumes that were each about 500 pages long. His brother, Charles Wesley, also traveled many miles on horseback and made good use of his time as well, having written over 5,000 hymns.

Horses know the way home and so do the angels. When a Christian dies and leaves this world, it is their angel who escorts them to their eternal home in Heaven.

The time came when the beggar died and the angels carried him to Abraham's side. The rich man also died and was buried (Luke 16:22 NIV).

In this statement, by Jesus we see the Lord confirming a truth that had been widely understood by the Jews, which is that the angels carry the righteous to Heaven at their death. Angels are ministering spirits, and since they help us here in the earth, they are also prepared to take us home to Heaven when it comes time for us to leave this planet.

Angels and horses do have a lot in common. By recognizing these similarities I believe we can be better prepared to work in harmony with the increased release of angelic help that the Lord is sending to His saints worldwide. The great harvest of souls that is at hand requires all hands on deck, and we need to be open in our understanding of the ministry that the angels bring to assist us.

Chapter Seven

ARE YOU A WAR HORSE
OR A SHOW HORSE?

ARE YOU A WAR HORSE
OR A SHOW HORSE?

Most of the horses mentioned in the Bible refer to war horses. A war horse could possibly be considered one of the most majestic creatures in the animal kingdom. Beautiful renderings of horses in the Bible cause many Christians to believe that the horse is God's favorite animal. Some, however, contend that the gigantic dinosaur Job spoke of would be God's favorite, citing the following verse.

> ***Behold now behemoth***, *which I made with thee; he eateth grass as an ox. Lo now, his strength is in his loins, and his force is in the navel of his belly. He moveth his tail like a cedar: the sinews of his stones are wrapped together. His bones are as strong as pieces of brass; his bones are like bars of iron. He is the **chief** of the ways of God: he*

that made him can make his sword to approach unto him (Job 40:15-19).

It appears that Job was describing a very large sauropod type dinosaur, perhaps the recently discovered Sauroposeidon which was uncovered in Oklahoma. When the fossils of this animal were first noticed, the researchers thought they had come across a large petrified tree. However, it wasn't a tree but rather the vertebrate of the creature's neck! This dinosaur weighed in at 120,000 pounds and created a small seismic tremor when it walked. It is arguably the largest creature to ever walk the earth.

Some Bible teachers say this reference in the book of Job is describing a hippopotamus, but that isn't accurate because it says; *he moveth his tail like a cedar.* Hippos and elephants have small, skinny tails, but this animal had a neck and tail the size of a tree! The description, *he is the chief of the ways of God* can be a little misleading. The word *chief* that is used here does not mean favorite, but simply means *the largest and biggest.* While the behemoth ranks as the biggest, I still think the horse ranks at the top of God's overall favorite animal. After all, when the Lord returns to earth, He will be riding on a white horse.

> *I saw heaven standing open and there before me was a white horse, whose rider is called Faithful and True. With justice he judges and makes war. …The armies of heaven were following him, riding on white horses and dressed in fine linen, white and clean* (Revelation 19:11,14 NIV).

The Lord rides on a white horse, and we are going to ride with Him. There must be a little bit of horse lover in all of us! When He rides into battle His animal of choice is one that matches the Lord's own glorious and majestic persona. The only animal qualified is the war horse. A war horse is able to pick up on his rider's emotions of courage and bravery and feeds off that emotional high, creating a frenzied state of explosive energy within the horse.

> *Hast thou given the horse strength? Hast thou clothed his neck with thunder? Canst thou make him afraid as a grasshopper? The glory of his nostrils is terrible. He paweth in the valley, and rejoiceth in his strength: he goeth on to meet the armed men. He mocketh at fear, and is not affrighted; neither turneth he back from the sword. The quiver rattleth against him, the glittering spear and the shield, He swalloweth the ground with fierceness and rage: neither believeth he that it is the sound of the trumpet. He saith among the trumpets, Ha, ha; and he smelleth the battle afar off, the thunder of the captains, and the shouting* (Job 39:19-25).

The war horse represents in many ways the *mature* Christian, who exemplifies the strong traits associated with the inward development of Christian character, while exhibiting an extreme level of devotion to the Lord. Maturity in Christ does not necessarily correspond with how long a person has been in the Church. Some Christians have been in the Church for decades, but still are hesitant to completely abandon their self life to the Lord. A war horse Christian is often viewed as being extreme or fanatical in the eyes of the show horse Christian, who is primarily concerned about being the center of attention and gaining the approval of man. There is a vast difference between a war horse Christian and a show horse Christian.

In 1990, I had a very enjoyable life while in college. Everybody liked me, and I had a lot of friends. I was the song leader for a college group of about 300 students that was the university outreach program to a large mainline denomination church of several thousand members, I had grown up in this denomination and always went to church whenever the doors were open. I am thankful that I was raised in church and got saved through a church youth camp. The only regret is that the church I belonged to as a whole never moved past the basic message of salvation and water baptism into the fullness of God's plan to grow and mature into spiritual adulthood.

This hindrance in spiritual growth produced some strange and unbiblical teachings within the church denomination. For instance, it is taught that only people who are members of this denomination are saved! Many of these dear people have been taught from the pulpit that they are the only ones going to Heaven. Growing up within this church I was also wrongly informed that you can't worship with instrumental music, and that God no longer performs miracles of any kind.

This spiritually dry climate was influenced by foul religious spirits, which produced a barren wasteland in my heart. Yet, this experience actually had a reverse effect on me, and I'm sure many others as well. The dryness made me extremely thirsty and made me want to escape to a place in God—full of life and fruitfulness.

While in college, every Sunday morning and Wednesday night I would lead the singing for the university group. We all had a lot of fun, and life was carefree and easy. As a senior, most of the younger students looked up to me as a leader and example to follow. It felt good having others admire me; I was enjoying the limelight of being a show horse.

The Lord has always given me a smile on my face; so I have always looked happy. Yet, on the inside I was struggling with knowing that I was not living a life that was pleasing to the Lord. While in church I looked like I had my act together, but in my heart I was grieved because of habitual sins that I found impossible to lay down. While everyone, including the campus pastoral staff, thought I was great, there was a secret cry of my heart that desired a real experience with God and freedom from controlling habits. One day, the Lord answered my prayer in a way that changed the course of my life.

QUENCHING THE THIRST

While walking from my apartment to the college campus one morning to attend my first class, I happened to see a bookstore that was on the street corner by the university. Because I love to read, I couldn't resist dropping in for a quick look around. To my surprise, it was a Christian bookstore. As I looked at some of the books, a man in his late twenties came over to assist me. As we talked he told me that the bookstore adjoined another building, which was used as a meeting place for a Charismatic church. He told me he was the pastor and he kindly invited me to visit sometime.

I decided to attend a Wednesday night meeting, and I enjoyed the lively praise and worship and was uplifted by the good preaching that ministered a refreshing word to me. After a few weeks I was attending on a regular basis. It's true what the old-timers say about the Pentecostal experience. That if you stand on the bank of the river long enough, eventually you will slip in.

After about two weeks, the pastor asked during church if there was anyone present who would like to receive the

baptism in the Holy Spirit with the evidence of speaking in tongues. I went forward along with another young woman who was about my age. As soon as the pastor laid his hands on my head a new language instantly began to flow up from my spirit and out of my mouth, and I began to speak in tongues. It felt so good to speak in tongues; up until that time I had never experienced a refreshing like that before.

To my right, I noticed a bit of a disturbance going on with the girl who also came forward. She was crying and kept saying, "It's not working. It's not working." For some reason she could not speak in tongues, and she appeared to be upset at the pastor because of this. I determined not to be distracted so I kept on praying in tongues, and continued praying in tongues after I left the church and after I got home. The experience was so precious to me that I prayed almost three days in tongues without stopping, except for times of sleeping and eating.

About two weeks later, I found out the girl next to me that night when I was filled with the Spirit was involved in a long-term adulterous relationship with a married man. She soon left the church because she was unwilling to forsake her sin. The Holy Spirit will fill us when we yield fully to Him.

After my experience of being filled with the Holy Spirit, I went back to my regular church and was so excited to tell them that miracles are still happening today. I was so sure they would be just as excited as I was, but I was met with blank stares and an overall cold reception. After a few visits, I got the message that I was no longer welcome. I told the university pastor how puzzled I was because when I lived with secret sins, I was warmly embraced; but when I wanted to live a holy life and be more pleasing to the Lord, I became an outcast. He never really answered my question, and responded by saying, "Oh, it's just normal to sin, everybody does it."

I also suffered persecution from my family who were convinced I had lost my mind when I told them I had been filled with the Holy Spirit and now spoke with heavenly tongues. When the issue of my mental sanity was further questioned, I confessed that their assertions were most likely correct. I told them, "It is true I have lost my mind. Thank God, I needed to lose that dirty thing! Now I have received the mind of Christ, and I'm working on renewing it daily with the Word of God."

Even though I was offered fully paid visits to see the best psychiatrist in town, I gladly turned them down. For the first time in my life, my spiritual vision was seeing beyond the elementary and basic truths of salvation and water baptism. There is so much more that God wants us to experience. A show horse tries to avoid persecution by attempting to please everybody. But if you are living right then you are bound to have some people get upset at you. That's because a godly man or woman carries the Presence of God, and it convicts those who want to live in sin and just camp out in a certain place in God and never go any further. There will be times when people get upset at you even when you have done nothing wrong. Even though there is no justifiable cause for them to persecute you they sometimes still lash out.

> **They that hate me without a cause** *are more than the hairs of mine head* (Psalm 69:4a).

A show horse is *not* a fitting representation for someone who wants to go deeper in their walk with God. When a believer surrenders their heart fully to the Lord then God is able to work in a developmental way that nurtures us into a place

of a true Father and child relationship. A genuine father who truly loves his child will be highly interested in seeing his child mature into adulthood. The father does not want the child to remain a child. Even as we mature into the stature of a mature man in Christ there are still areas of refining within us that God is constantly working on.

WALKING INTO MATURITY

I remember a time when I had stepped out into the full-time ministry, and things seemed to be moving along okay, until I hit some bumps in the road. Although I had started a television ministry within the city we lived by the Lord's leading, there were still not enough ministry engagements on my schedule to meet our financial needs. The Lord impressed upon my heart that I had to take on some extra work until my itinerant ministry was a little stronger.

Just like Paul had to make tents at times to make ends meet, the Lord also directed me to take a full-time job until a bigger wave of ministry engagements were scheduled. He encouraged me by telling me that the season of having to go back to work would be short and that He would make it as smooth as possible. I replied to the Lord, "Lord, I've started a television ministry in this city and have been on the air for several months. People will recognize me as a television minister if I go to apply for a job."

The idea of going from recording a television show twice a week in a beautiful television studio in a city of over one million people, to having to work a "normal" job was a tough pill to swallow for the remaining remnants of the show-horse mentality lingering in me. But the Lord was masterfully chipping away my pride and self-preservation with the skill of a

Master Artisan. Despite my pleas, I knew in my heart that I would have to step back from devoting my sole attention to the ministry and obtain a good job until the Lord opened enough ministry doors that it was impossible for me to work in another job.

Because I had plumbing experience and had also previously worked for a home improvement store, I went to the local home improvement store and applied for a job. This was a different store from the one I had previously worked at, but it was with the same nationwide company. After having filled out the on-line application from my home computer, I called the store manager and set up an appointment.

As I drove to the store, I tried to reassure myself that out of a city so large, surely no one would recognize me as one of those "television ministers." It wasn't that I was ashamed of the gospel, but rather I felt embarrassed about going from celebrity mode to normal mode. As I walked up to the office, I was just about to tell the secretary that I had an appointment, when suddenly her eyes got real big and she said, "You're that guy on television! My son watches you all the time." She said it so loud that everybody within a 15-foot radius stopped and looked over at me.

Then the worst case scenario that I could have imagined took place. With everybody looking at me, she said, "What are you here for?" Swallowing every ounce of pride within me, I quietly said, "I'm here to apply for a job." When I said that, everyone who was listening went back to their work. I was taken to the manager's office, and I had a few minutes of privacy before the manager arrived. As I was quietly talking to the Lord, I said, "Lord, I can't believe you did that to me out there. That was embarrassing." The Lord replied by speaking with love and firmness, "I never called you to be a show horse; I called you to be a war horse."

As I faithfully worked as a "plumbing specialist," God blessed my work, and it was never stressful or over-demanding. The store manager was very happy to have me onboard. He even confided in me that he had been a former missionary in South East Asia for several years. He was a Spirit-filled believer, and he understood my situation. There was a point one time, however, when I did have a little bit of difficulty with my department manager.

I had only been there one week, and he was being rude and nasty with me because he was having a strenuous time dealing with some personal issues, which were producing a lot of stress in his life. I did not respond negatively or retaliate with sharp words. I just kept on doing my work of stacking toilets on the toilet aisle. While I was lifting an empty stacking pallet up off the floor, he suddenly stopped and said, "You look just like that minister on television." I said, "I'm the man." The biggest smile broke out on his face, and he said, "Praise God! I'm a Southern Baptist, and I watch you on television every week! I'm so glad you're here, if there's anything I can do for you please let me know."

From that day on, my job was a total cakewalk. Soon, word spread through the whole store that I was a minister. I almost never had a free moment in the break room to myself, as people were always asking me questions about the Lord or sharing their requests with me for prayer. It was one of the most humbling, as well as spiritually productive experiences in my life. I thank God that He allowed me to go through such a season, in which He melted out of me any desire to crave an elite, show-horse lifestyle. After a short four months at this job, the Lord returned me to full-time ministry.

There's nothing wrong with being on television, radio, or any other form of media outreach. These are ministry tools that are necessary in preaching the gospel. When a person is called into the public ministry, then at times it means public exposure, sometimes on a grand scale. These things are fine, but it is the lust for power and prestige that the Holy Spirit wants us to keep ourselves pure from. We should be willing to work any job or do anything that God asks of us. The greatest job or the greatest assignment that a person could ever do is to perform the task that God specifically directs *you* to do.

A war horse Christian is not interested in being on the Who's Who list of the most popular Christians. Nor are they hung up on having to be recognized with a lofty title. Once I was ministering at a well-known church in Southern California, and I was talking to the pastor's wife before I was to go up on the platform to minister. She asked me how I wanted to be introduced to the people, and I said, "Just announce me as Brother Steven."

When I said that she appeared startled and replied, "You mean, I don't have to call you the Supreme Bishop, or Your Holy Revered Highness like most of the other ministers want to be addressed?"

I said, "No, Brother Steven will be fine."

She said, "Thank God, the title game was beginning to nauseate me."

Now this doesn't mean we should ever disrespect a minister. A minister of the gospel should be honored, and titles are

fine and are fitting to bestow honor. But they should not be demanded, or used to elevate a person to a position of deity.

In contrast to a show-horse Christian, the war-horse Christian is someone who simply accepts his or her assignment from God and is happy at heart to fulfill that task. Such a person works with diligence and is aware that their conduct is being watched by those who are looking for someone who doesn't just put on a good talk, but demonstrates Christian character on a consistent basis. The war-horse Christian has a burden for lost souls and wants to see the Church rise to her place of authority and righteous influence in the earth.

The war-horse minister is not mesmerized by glitz and glitter, but walks in love toward the rich and poor alike. Such a minister may have great notoriety, or may be hidden for the Lord's purposes. The war-horse minister does not water down the Full Gospel message, but teaches the whole Bible, even if some subjects are not politically correct. The war-horse minister is not afraid of the devil because he or she understands their authority in Christ. The war-horse minister is not a coward or someone who apologizes for what the Bible says, but is a person who is full of faith and power in God.

"HE WUZ DA MOSTEST HOSS!"

In these days when God is calling us to run with the horses, we can find inspiration when we look at how God worked through one of His special creations, a horse that is considered to be the most well-known thoroughbred of all time.

Hold your strength till the barriers fly,
Then close with the leaders eye to eye.
Thundering hooves and the mad jammed race,

Blood in the nostrils, sweat in the face.
And children, remember wherever you are,
You carry the blood of Man O' War.
(Anonymous)

Man O' War was born in 1917 in Kentucky, where the greatest race horses often come from. He was one of 1,680 thoroughbreds foaled that year, but God graced this horse with a special touch. He was purchased for $5,000 from his breeder in 1917 by Sportsman Samuel Riddle. Soon thereafter Man O' War grew to be a huge horse weighing over 1,100 pounds and standing 16 $1/2$ hands tall. His girth was 72" across, and he also ate more than other horses. Each day he ate 12 quarts of oats, while most racehorses only ate 9 quarts. His stride was incredible, measuring from 25 to 28 feet.

Man O' War possessed such a fiery spirit that in the beginning it was difficult to bridle and saddle him. His owner took efforts to see that his special horse's burning spirit was never quenched, but rather guarded and respected. A stable boy once said about Man O' War, "He's nice and he's smart, but don't ever try to force him or you'll come out second best every time. Ask him and he'll do what you want. Push him and it's all off."

Man O' War began his racing career on June 6, 1919, as a two-year-old. He went to the post 21 times and won 20 races. In his first race at Belmont he won by six lengths, even when his rider pulled up on the reins slowing Man O' War to a literal canter. The jockey stood straight up in his stirrups and looked back at the field as he crossed the finish line in ease. In reporting this race, the *New York Morning Telegraph* reported: "He made a half dozen high-class youngsters look like $200 horses." Three weeks later he won the Keene Memorial Stakes.

In the early 1900s, there were no starting gates like we use today. The jockeys at that time would circle their horses around and ride them up to the line and wait for the starter to wave a flag to begin the race. Man O' War's only loss came at the Sanford Memorial Stakes as he was still circling with his back to the starting line when the flag was dropped. After the jockey got Man O' War turned around, the pack was already off and running at full speed. Man O' War charged at a tremendous pace and caught and passed the pack and was closing on the leader but ran out of time, as a horse named Upset crossed the finish line first, only a half a length in front of Man O' War. This was the only race Man O' War ever lost, and it coined a new term in the sports world—*Upset* now denotes a surprise victory over the one expected to win. Man O' War went on to defeat Upset every time he raced him.

Man O' War did not just win races, but he dominated them with amazing ease. He didn't just shave time off of existing records, he smashed them. In one race at Belmont Park in 1920, he won by 100 lengths! He carried as much as 138 pounds, while conceding as much as 30 pounds to his rivals and still beat them by wide margins. His presence seemed to guarantee unprecedented attendance because he had a way of electrifying racing fans. Security details had to be enacted to protect the horse from fans pulling keepsake hairs from his body. Even detectives were assigned to protect the horse against several threats made against him from those who did not like him winning all the time. His owner ran him in every major race except for the Kentucky Derby, which he deemed the horse to be too young in his bone development at that early stage of his life.

Man O' War's track records stood for many years until the development of aluminum racing shoes and improved track racing surfaces. His last official race was run in October 1920 after his owner decided it would hurt the horse to carry the every increasing handicap weight that was being assigned to him. He was so superior to other horses of his time that the Jockey Club handicapper said he would put more weight on him than any horse had ever carried as a four year old. Rather than risk a breakdown under ridiculously heavy weights, his owner opted to retire him after his three-year campaign.

In 1920, Texas oil man and millionaire, William Waggoner, offered to buy Man O' War for $500,000. The owner of Man O' War, Samuel Riddle, turned down the offer. Shortly thereafter, Waggoner upped his offer to $1 million. Again Riddle refused to sell. "Well, how much then?" asked Waggoner.

"The colt is not for sale," insisted Riddle. Waggoner then signed a blank check that Riddle could fill in for whatever amount he so desired. But Riddle responded to Waggoner saying, "You go to France and bring back the sepulcher of Napoleon from Les Invalides. Then you go to England and buy the jewels from the crown. Then to India and buy the Taj Mahal. Then I'll put a price on Man O' War." Certainly he was a horse whose worth exceeded monetary value.

Even in his last race he defeated, by seven lengths, the great Sir Barton, who was a previous Triple Crown champion. In retirement Man O' War continued to set records by siring champions. Of the almost 400 foals that he sired, more than 200 of them became champions in their own right. One of them was War Admiral who became the 1938 Triple Crown winner. Man O' War went on to live to be 30 years of age.

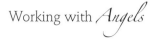

In 1999, the *Blood-Horse Magazine* assembled a panel of seven of the world's leading horse experts to choose the top 100 thoroughbred racing horses of the 20th century. *The Blood-Horse Magazine* is an international weekly news magazine about thoroughbred horses and racing that was founded in 1916. It is considered to be the number one magazine of its kind in the world. Out of the 100 greatest thoroughbred champions of the 20th century, *Man O' War was chosen as the greatest horse of all.*

During his stud days, Man O' War had a special relationship with his life-long groomer, who was a precious African-American man named Will Harbut. As horseracing fans would often come out to see the big horse on the farm, it was Will Harbut who would show the stallion, and he would always say, *"He wuz da mostest hoss!"* Many say the bond between Will and Man O' War was so strong that when Will died, Man O' War died from a broken heart because he couldn't stand to be without his best friend. Man O' War died barely a month after Will died. Will Harbut had 12 children, and one of his son's actually went on to exercise ride War Admiral and War Relic, both descendants of Man O' War.

I don't think it's any coincidence that the horse considered to be the greatest of all time has such a fitting name as Man O' War. God is looking for those who will rise up with the same spirit as Man O' War and go forth and accomplish great works in the name of Jesus. We serve a supernatural God who is able to move upon us by His Spirit and empower us to run with the horses, and beyond. Don't allow yourself to be held back by settling for a show horse lifestyle where all you do is sit around and look at yourself in the mirror and say, "I'm glad I'm blessed, and that's all that really matters."

Rise up and smell the battle. Stir yourself to face the enemy. If God is for us then who can be against us? The victory is ours in Christ Jesus. As you obey the plan of God for your life, I believe the war-horse anointing will come upon you in power, and you will run the race that God has set before you with fire and passion, just as Man O' War did in his day and time.

It's interesting to see the prophetic indicators exemplified in Man O' War's life. While researching about this horse, I discovered that certain writers who witnessed Man O' War's races wrote that he had every resemblance of a war horse. It is that same anointing and strength of the war horse that God is releasing to His people today.

Like Man O' War, we can receive wisdom to avoid unpleasant upsets. Historical records indicate that the starter who dropped the starting flag when Man O' War was not yet in position to race, did so on purpose to hinder Man O' War from winning. There are many people of lesser spiritual values who would love to see us fail, but if we stay prayed up and keep our eyes on Jesus, then we will not be caught off guard, and we will come out on top at the finish line.

It greatly blessed my heart to see how Man O' War's owner could not be bought out with money. Many ministers have compromised their integrity and their high calling because of their love for money. Some pastors are afraid to preach on the Baptism in the Holy Spirit with the evidence of speaking in tongues because they are afraid they will upset certain church members who may withhold their giving. This kind of compromise is wrong, and a man or woman of God should not allow themselves to be manipulated because of money.

While we understand that God wants us to prosper, we should not run after money. The blessings of God should run after us and chase us down as we walk closely with the Lord and not back down from preaching the whole-Gospel message, which includes divine healing and God's miracle power for us today.

The relationship between Will Harbut and Man O' War also demonstrates the deep bonding that comes from a genuine love and mutual respect between two friends. As we have seen, angels are likewise attracted to environments of peace, uplifting words, and an attitude of optimism. This is something we can be mindful of and endeavor to emulate.

The Lord also desires us to be spiritually reproductive just as Man O' War sired many other champions after his racing career was completed. We have a responsibility to reach out and help strengthen our weaker brothers and sisters in Christ. We should desire for other Christians to ascend with us to higher realms of understanding and wholeness in Christ.

In 1991, when another Christian I barely knew gave me a book by A.W. Tozer it triggered in me a greater desire to know God. Just reading that one book opened a whole new reality in my Christian walk that did not exist before. Giving an anointed book or a teaching CD is an eternal investment that could revolutionize someone's life. By our taking the time to care and place in the hands of others some tool of spiritual edification, we can be influential in reproducing more and more men, women, and children who know their God and are spiritually developed in Him.

Chapter Eight

ANGELS SENT FORTH

ANGELS SENT FORTH

Angels are ministering spirits that are sent forth from Heaven to serve believers in the earth. The subject of whether or not angels can be given commands or directives is a topic of much debate. The lowest common denominator question that people usually ask: "Can angels be given orders?" Well, the answer to that question is yes, and no.

No, because humans can't tell angels what to do, like, "Hey, you angels, get me a new car because I don't like the one I've got!" That is ridiculous, and I think most of God's people know better than that.

But yes, there can be times when it is necessary to speak directives to angels, but this must be done by the leading of the Holy Spirit. There can be times when the Holy Spirit can lead a believer to ask God the Father to dispatch angels, or even times when the Holy Spirit may lead a believer to speak an instruction directly to an angel, or angels. A person may then wonder how they are supposed to know what the right thing to do is. There are no clear-cut rules; it takes dependence on the Holy Spirit and learning as you go. There are no formulas to follow. What worked for one person may not work for you because the Holy Spirit may choose to do things differently through you than He did with someone else.

I have found it important to understand that the dividing line regarding speaking directives to angels is often only crossed by those who believe in a God who performs miracles today. A child of God must realize that the gifts of the Spirit are supernatural gifts.

> But the manifestation of the Spirit is given to each one for the profit of all: for to one is given the word of wisdom through the Spirit; to another the word of knowledge through the same Spirit, to another faith by the same Spirit, to another gifts of healings by the same Spirit, to another the working of miracles, to another prophecy, **to another discerning of spirits**, to another different kinds of tongues, to another the interpretation of tongues. But one and the same Spirit works all these things, distributing to each one as He wills (1 Corinthians 12:7-11 NKJV).

The gift of discerning of spirits is a manifestation of the Holy Spirit that allows a person to see, hear, smell, taste, or touch in the realm of the Spirit. Because some Christians have never experienced the Holy Spirit manifesting through them with the supernatural gift of discerning of spirits, they think the gift of discerning of spirits is referring to the ability of knowing if a person is nice, mean, trustworthy, unreliable, or possessing certain character traits. But being able to size a person up and get a good feel for the way they are is just simple discernment. That does not take a supernatural miracle.

However, when a child of God is experiencing a God-given vision, trance, or dream which takes them into the realm of the Spirit, then that is the gift of discerning of spirits in operation. This is why there is a major difference between doing something under the anointing of the Holy Spirit as compared to someone just trying something in the flesh while hoping to get some kind of result. If it is not empowered by the Holy Spirit then it will fall to the ground ineffective. While it is not always necessary for there to be a supernatural manifestation of the gifts of the Spirit before stepping out in faith to give angelic directives, there should be an anointing of the Holy Spirit that quickens us and stirs us to act in the way that we do. We can thank the Lord that we have an anointing within our hearts that teaches us regarding situations like these.

One of the wonderful characteristics about God is that He enjoys getting His people involved in His Kingdom activities. Sometimes our relationship with God is similar to a basketball game. If God were on a basketball team with most Christians, they would expect Him to take all the shots and make all the baskets. But it doesn't work that way in our walk with Him. Besides, that would be a pretty boring game. God wants everybody involved in the game. That's why many times He bounces the basketball right over to us and says, "Go ahead, you take the next shot!"

It always blesses me when I read about the miracles of Jesus recorded in the Gospels. Often times after a great miracle took place, Jesus would say to the recipient, "*Your faith* has made you whole." Some Christians try to put all the responsibility on

God, but Jesus knew the miracles He performed were done because someone had faith in God. Somebody didn't just sit back and expect God to do everything. Somebody got up and started moving toward God and combined their faith with corresponding works, and thus a miracle came forth. God expects us to be involved when it comes to working with angels. He has entrusted us with His authority, and Jesus can function through us in the earth because we are His Body, the Church.

A friend of mine had an interesting experience take place the night before 9-11-2001 that demonstrates how the Lord wants us to be involved in assigning angels to specific tasks. Almost everyone knows what happened on 9-11-2001—terrorists attacked the World Trade Center and the Pentagon by crashing passenger airplanes loaded with fuel into their targets causing the loss of over 3,000 lives. On the night before 9-11 at 3 o'clock in the morning, my friend was awakened by the hum of a great noise that sounded like many helicopters landing in the woods across from his home. He said he then heard singing that was like a beautiful, well-orchestrated mass choir. He recognized the sound to be a large group of angels that had just landed.

Suddenly, their beautiful singing turned to weeping, and it was then when the Holy Spirit spoke to him, saying, "Tonight, Israel is in the greatest danger it has ever been in. Dispatch the angels to go and form an umbrella of protection over Israel." That night he stayed up all night long asking God the Father to send the angels to Israel. Through his prayers he was able to dispatch wave after wave of angels to Israel to form an umbrella of protection over the entire nation.

Having stayed up all night in prayer, he turned on the television later that morning and saw the Twin Towers under attack.

It appears that the devil also had major plans to not only cause a terrorist attack to be launched in the United States, but wanted to inflict a potential rocket attack or nuclear blast upon Israel as well. My friend believes that he was not the only one who God spoke to that night to pray for Israel. He believes there were others who God directed to pray that angels be sent to Israel in order to shield Israel and thus avoid some form of devastating attack.

Angels beyond numbers are standing by waiting for dispatches and assignments, but are not sent forth because of misunderstandings concerning the ministry of angels. There have been countless angels left standing in the "unemployment line" that wanted to render aid or assistance, but they were never gainfully employed by believers. Some Christians question whether or not angels can be given directives. I believe that when many people get to Heaven, they will have to give account for their failure to utilize one of God's primary methods of helping the believer fulfill Kingdom agenda's in the earth.

Despite what some may think, there are far more angels than there are people. God is not in short supply of angels. Even though there are an estimated six billion people on this planet, there are far more angels. God has trillions of angels who have never entered service because they are waiting to be called up for assignment. Heaven's economy is unlimited and will never be exhausted by humans.

FAITH REQUIRED

Working with angels requires faith in God. Just because one cannot see an angel or feel the brushing of their wings does not mean they are not near. Many Christians are looking for spectacular manifestations while they consistently miss the simple, everyday supernatural workings of the Spirit of God.

Once, when my wife and I were going through a great financial struggle due to a bad financial decision I had made, there was a particular day that was quite difficult to get through. Of course, when you have no money every day is difficult: but this one day was very discouraging. We were living in a coastal city in Southern California at the time and had gone into town to pick up our mail at the post office. The entire morning my wife, Kelly, kept seeing large, white pickup trucks. I didn't think anything about it, although it was unusual to see pickups in this town because most people drove cars.

After checking our mail, we again were disappointed that some expected financial relief had not arrived. As we left the post office and pulled out into the street, Kelly spontaneously spoke out in a loud voice, "Why have I been seeing all of these large, white pickup trucks?" As soon as she said that I had to slow down as I pulled up to a red traffic light. At the same time, two very large, white pickup trucks pulled up next to us, one on each side of our car.

We were both amazed, and we felt that God was trying to speak to us somehow. Later that day while in prayer, I was talking to the Lord about our difficult situation, and He spoke to my heart saying, "I have assigned two very large angels who are robed in white to help deliver you from your distress. They will be with you until you are back on your feet again."

Although I never saw two angels, the two white pickup trucks were symbolic of the two angels who were assigned to help deliver us in our time of need. I certainly benefited from their help as God made a way for us when there was no way out in the natural. After three months we were back on our feet again with a new job for me and a beautiful home that was supernaturally made available for us. Many times the Lord drops divine hints and seemingly unusual coincidences to actually give us prophetic indicators of His nearness, as well as the closeness of the angels.

There are several Scriptures that provide insight and a biblical foundation when it comes to speaking God-given directives to angels. One passage that I have always enjoyed is found in Psalm 103:

> *Bless the LORD, you His angels, Who excel in strength, who do His word, Heeding the voice of His word. Bless the LORD, all you His hosts, You ministers of His, who do His pleasure* (Psalm 103:20-21 NKJV).

The key phrase that refers to giving directives to angels is, *"Heeding the voice of His word."* To *heed* means "to hear and obey." Angels respond to the anointed, living Word of God. Notice it does not say, "Heeding the voice of the Lord." Of course, angels always obey the Lord, but they will also heed the Word of God when it is spoken under the anointing and power of the Spirit. Our words have creative power whether we realize it or not.

Humans were created just slightly lower than God and our words frame the world that we choose to live in. The words that come out of our mouths have the power of life and death. As we give voice to the Word of God, angels go forth to move on our behalf according to the will of God.

The Word of God will not speak on its own. That may surprise some people, but it is true. Your Holy Bible can lie on your coffee table for ten silent years and never speak a word—unless you open it up and give voice to it. Angels heed the voice of His Word. If you speak the Word of God under the anointing of the Holy Spirit then angels respond. Now, I'm not talking about speaking just any verse in the Bible. It must be a living Word that God speaks to you. If it is not a rhema (living) Word, then it is only an intellectual exercise. We must be willing to go past mental reasoning and move into spiritual enlightenment. Head knowledge is good and has its proper place in Bible study, but only the *living* Word of God that illumines our hearts will produce victory and cause spiritual progress.

Angels respond to the anointed, living Word of God. They will heed what you say because you are an extension, a mouthpiece, of the Word of God.

In October 2003, I received a visitation from the Lord that helped me better understand how He uses His angels to give heed to the anointed words we speak. In October, most people are beginning to plan for Thanksgiving and Christmas. At this time, my wife and I were still barely making enough money to cover bills and necessary expenses. Thanksgiving would not be a problem for us because all of Kelly's relatives lived nearby, and one of her sisters was going to host the family Thanksgiving meal at her home. But Christmas was a different story. Although my confessions of faith centered on abundance and a full supply, we were faced with having no extra money to buy Christmas gifts. I had told the Lord in prayer that I needed His help regarding this situation.

One morning that month, I was alone praying in the bedroom of our home. My wife and daughter were visiting a nearby relative, so I had the house to myself. I started praying around 8 A.M. and had a wonderful time in prayer until I stopped at just a few minutes past 10 A.M. I was about to get up from praying to do some work outside when I sensed in my spirit that a supernatural visitation was about to happen. Through this experience I think I now have a better understanding of what David encountered when the Lord spoke specific instructions to him in one particular military campaign.

> *As soon as you hear the sound of marching in the tops of the balsam trees, move out to battle, because that will mean that God has gone out in front of you to strike the Philistine army* (1 Chronicles 14:15 NIV).

David was told to listen for a sound in the tops of the trees that would indicate angelic presence; it was most likely a large army of warrior angels who had come to help him and his men defeat the Philistines.

STRETCHING FORTH

That morning, as I sensed a tremendous surge of spiritual activity, I immediately got back down on my knees and began to pray in tongues. As I did, I looked up and saw the Lord Jesus walk right through the back wall of my bedroom and come and stand about five feet in front of me. He was accompanied by an angel dressed in white.

As I looked at the Lord, I saw Him dressed as a Shepherd from head to toe. He looked as if He had been out on a field taking care of sheep. I've known through Bible study that He is the Lord our Shepherd, but it was different seeing Him like this in real life. He wore a long shepherd's garment that appeared well worn by exposure to sun and rain. His head was wrapped with a protective shawl, although His bearded chin and face were uncovered. He had leather sandals on His feet that were a light tan color. As He stood there in His shepherd garments, I couldn't help but notice that He also held a shepherd's rod in his right hand.

The rod was even curved at the top in order to reach out and grab a wandering sheep around the neck and gently pull it in. The interesting thing about His rod is that I knew it represented authority, but the color of the rod was white, and it had bright, red stripes encircling it from top to bottom. It actually looked like a very large candy cane. In my heart, I knew the Lord wanted me and my family to have a good Christmas.

As I stood up and faced the Lord, He extended His rod toward me while His facial expression implied that He had confidence in me that I would respond correctly. With my right hand I reached out and took hold of the rod. I held the rod in the air with the hooked end extending outward in order to pull in what I would grasp. With a surge of Holy Spirit boldness I extended the rod outward and said, "Money, come, to me, now!" I said this three times, each time very forcefully. As I spoke those words, I would swing that shepherd's rod out and by faith grab hold of money by the hook at the end of the staff, and then pull it in.

This may seem strange, but in the Old Testament when King Joash of Israel needed deliverance from the king of Aram, we see the Prophet Elisha telling King Joash to shoot an arrow out of the window as a prophetic act of the Lord's deliverance. King Joash was then instructed by Elisha to strike the arrows to the ground.

> *Then he said, "Take the arrows," and the king took them. Elisha told him, "Strike the ground." He struck it three times and stopped* (2 Kings 13:18 NIV).

To *strike the ground* could be better translated as to "shoot to the ground." Elisha was speaking forth a supernatural word of wisdom that had the potential to bring complete victory to Israel. He was instructing King Joash to shoot arrows from the window by his bed into the ground outside, just as if he were shooting against a real enemy.

This event was beyond that of a symbolic act. The Holy Spirit opened up the supernatural realm to King Joash through the Prophet Elisha's ministry. Every battle that is ever won must first be won in the realm of the spirit. Every living Word that God speaks to us has the ability to produce the desired request, but it must be mixed with faith. King Joash was carried into the realm of the Spirit by riding on the anointing of Elisha, but once there, he had to act for himself.

> *The man of God was angry with him and said, "You should have struck the ground five or six times; then you would have defeated Aram and completely destroyed it. But now you will defeat it only three times* (2 Kings 13:19 NIV).

Elisha was very upset with King Joash's lazy and half-hearted effort. The king's unbelief and spiritually-lethargic attitude cost Israel the total freedom that God desired for His people to have. When you have an open Heaven, you've got to go for it and not hold back. It's not every day that God grants such marvelous opportunities.

After I stretched forth the Lord's rod three times to pull in much needed provision, I stopped and handed the shepherd's rod back to the Lord. I sensed in my heart that three times was all that was necessary. As I handed the candy-cane colored shepherd's rod back to Him, He had a smile on His face that spoke more than words. Actually, He never spoke a single word to me during the entire visitation. Words are not always necessary. Sometimes the language of faith includes silence. The expression of, "Well done!" was written all over His face. He looked at me with a smile, and then He and the angel departed as the vision lifted from me.

That Christmas turned out to be a wonderful time for me and my family. Unexpected financial blessings came in to us through many different avenues. The Lord moved upon the hearts of our covenant partners in ministry and through some good, unexpected year-end church meetings which allowed me to earn considerable extra money. We were able to buy gifts for all of our more than 30 relatives, and bless our own children with what they wanted for Christmas.

I remember taking communion on Christmas morning with my family and realizing what a miracle the Lord had done for us financially. A few days after Christmas, I was in prayer, and I asked the Lord about the angel who appeared with Him that day when He visited me in October. The Lord said, "As you spoke that day to the money and called it in, he is the angel who went forth and caused it to come."

This experience is only one example of how angels heed the voice of His Word. As we speak the words that His Spirit puts in our mouth, we speak with authority, and the Kingdom of Heaven backs us up.

The Scripture that I believe sheds the most light on this subject of giving directives to angels is found in the Book of Hebrews.

> *Are they not all ministering spirits, sent forth to minister for them who shall be heirs of salvation?* (Hebrews 1:13).

This verse reveals that angels are ministering spirits. The word *minister* simply means "one who serves." Angels *serve* those who shall be heirs of salvation. Any born-again Christian will be an heir of salvation. Although we are saved when we put our faith and trust in Jesus, it is not until we finally get to Heaven that we realize the full extent of our salvation.

The human spirit is recreated by God when a person receives Jesus as their Lord and Savior. Along with the spirit, the mind and body also comprise the makeup of who we are as living human beings. Although our inward being has been born again, we will continually be renewing our mind with the Word of God as long as we are on this earth. Our minds have not been fully redeemed yet and neither have our bodies.

When we get to Heaven, we will receive a new glorified body that will overtake our resurrected physical bodies with immortality. When we get to Heaven, our minds will acclimate to the clear knowledge of God's Word. Our full salvation will then be complete, and we will live forever with our Lord. I'm excited just thinking about it!

While on the earth, though, we have the angels at our service to carry out the will of God. Jesus had the angels at His service as well when He conducted His earthly ministry. Some Christians may say, "Well sure He did, He was Jesus!" While Jesus was fully God on the earth, He laid down His mighty power and operated as a normal man who was reliant upon the Holy Spirit. The only distinct difference about Jesus is that He was filled with the Spirit without measure; and we as children of God are filled with a *measure* of God's Spirit.

We have all been given a measure of faith within our hearts. Jesus had to lay down His mighty power and operate

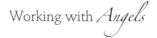

as a man or the devil would have proclaimed to God, "No fair, He's cheating." Satan swindled Adam out of the authority originally given to him by God. Adam was a man, and whoever was going to take the authority back which satan held after the Fall, it would have to be a man. That is why Jesus is referred to in the Bible as the *second Adam*. He won back what the first Adam originally lost. Jesus was qualified to do this because He came into the earth as a man.

If Jesus, as a man, had angels who could respond to His call, then so do we. But remember, Jesus was reliant totally upon the guidance and leading of the Holy Spirit. He didn't constantly tell angels what to do. For carnal Christians, this area of temptation will never have to be faced since this level of Kingdom authority only comes to those who have reached a very mature stage of sonship in God. No parent in their right mind would give a child a loaded gun. In the same way, God will not entrust an untrained and unqualified Christian who is still in the early stages of character development with real heavenly power. To do so would destroy a person. Jesus was an obedient Son who would not yield to the devil's temptation to demonstrate His authority over the angels, nor was Jesus interested in having the approval of His status as the Son of God being confirmed by a rogue, outlaw spirit.

> *Then the devil took him to the holy city and had him stand on the highest point of the temple. "If you are the Son of God," he said, "throw yourself down. For it is written: 'He will command his angels concerning you, And they will lift you up in their hands, so that you will not strike your foot against a stone.'" Jesus answered him, "It is also written, 'Do not put the Lord your God to the test'"* (Matthew 4:5-7 NIV).

We can see through this example that we must trust the Holy Spirit to lead us when it comes to giving directives to angels. Jesus Himself said He could have called in a vast angelic army during His betrayal in the garden, but He did not do it because it was His Father's will for Him to suffer and die upon the Cross to redeem humankind.

> *"Do you think I cannot call on my Father, and he will at once put at my disposal more than twelve legions of angels?"* (Matthew 26:53 NIV).

Jesus could have asked His Father for help and immediately had over 72,000 angels show up. The phrase *at my disposal* indicates that Jesus had authority to give specific instructions to the angels—should He deem it necessary. When Jesus rose from the dead, He delegated His authority to the Church that we may also utilize the resources of Heaven while here on the earth.

There is order and rank in God's Kingdom. Working with angels is not about showing off, it's simply about getting a job done. Angels are here to serve for us, so we should be alert for Spirit-led opportunities to employ the angels. There are times when the Holy Spirit will impress upon our hearts to speak to the angels that they might be sent forth to cause assignments to be accomplished. Should this be the case, we should give voice to His Word that the angels may respond and do the will of God.

TO THEM AND FOR THEM

The writer of Hebrews comes forward with a question about angels that generates an affirmative response by saying, "Are they not all ministering spirits, sent forth to minister *for them* who shall be heirs of salvation?" The term *for them* is useful in understanding one of the methods by which

angels can be put into action on our behalf. Regarding the angels, notice that this verse does not say, "...sent forth to minister *to* them." But rather, it says, "...sent forth to minister *for* them." If the angels only served *to us* then all we would have to do is sit back and relax and not do anything.

The word *to* can be defined as being "specifically directed toward," which implies that the angels are already busy serving a person. That would be nice, but let us not forget that God takes pleasure in our involvement in matters of the Kingdom. The words *for them*, or *for us* if we personalize it, indicates a different picture. The English word *for* denotes "on the behalf of." When we realize that the angels are sent to serve on our behalf, then in my understanding of the English language, that implies our need to help direct things. If somebody doesn't step up and give some directions, then everybody just stands around doing nothing.

When on construction sites, I have noticed how the foreman directs the progress of the work being done. While many times he doesn't have to say anything to the workers because they already know what to do, he may, however, find it necessary to give directions to a new group of subcontractors who have recently arrived at the job site. These subcontractors need to know what's going on.

Angels are constantly traveling back and forth from Heaven to earth. When Jacob had the vision of the angels descending and ascending on the ladder that reached from Heaven to earth, he obviously saw the tremendous amount of activity that takes place in the spirit realm that we are unaware of with our human eyes. We need to be on the ball just like a good foreman who is endeavoring to complete a job on time. If new angels arrive on the scene to render help, then we need to let them know what to do.

When Kelly and I were first married, we would at times pick up extra work by taking jobs in the banquet catering business. These jobs revolved around a team serving large groups, of sometimes a thousand people, with a full-course meal in a beautiful setting. Each banquet server had a very large tray that made it possible to stack about 20 hot meals in covered dishes that came from the kitchen pre-plated and ready to serve the guests. We took the meals from the kitchen and served **to** the people. We served **to** them because the meals were already prepared, and there was no other selection available. The selection of food had been chosen several weeks in advance by the banquet manager and the person reserving the facilities. That is why we served **to** them. *Some Things Are already predetermined By ~~Us~~ By God That Angels Are to do —*

A restaurant setting is different than a catered banquet. In a catered banquet one serve's **to** the guest. In a restaurant, the server serves **for** the guest. He or she serves **for** the guest because the server does not know what we want to eat. She takes our order and then sees to it that we get what we asked for. When the order is ready, the server brings it to the table **for** us. If a person went to a restaurant and never placed an order, it is doubtful if any food would arrive. It is the customer's responsibility to tell the server what we want to eat and how we want it prepared. Eggs and beef can be prepared in a variety of ways. If instructions aren't given, the customer will be stuck with whatever the cook decides. *Some Things you get To pick from The Menu which Are predetermined*

Similar to the way a server at a restaurant serves **for** you, the Word of God says that angels are, "sent forth to minister **for** them who shall be heirs of salvation." As the Holy Spirit leads, be attentive to give specific directions to angels in order to progress and expedite the plan and perfect will of God for your life.

Chapter Nine

THE LOST KEY
TO VICTORY

THE LOST KEY TO VICTORY

Because angels are heavenly messengers, it is possible that there can be times when the Lord sends His angels to us to reveal hidden secrets and unravel mysteries of spiritual truth. Years back, I remember reading the first verse of Psalm 34 and making a commitment to the Lord to obey this verse even when it proved difficult.

> *I will bless the LORD* **at all times**: *his praise shall* **continually** *be in mouth* (Psalm 34:1).

I determined in my heart that I was going to praise the Lord in good times or challenging times, in times of blessing and times of trouble. That doesn't mean we praise God for bad things, it simply means that we praise God because He is greater than any problem, and He can work through any situation when we love and praise Him. Soon after making that

commitment, I was faced with some good opportunities to grumble and complain rather than praise; but the Lord strengthened me to praise Him instead of yielding to the lower nature. The Lord began to teach me a valuable lesson about the benefits of praising Him when I was working in the plumbing field.

I worked with Bill, my father-in-law, and Jeff, my brother-in-law. Kelly's father taught me the skills necessary to be a good plumber. One day we were working on a historical home in Southern California that was 100 years old and needed a complete re-piping job on all of the plumbing. A re-pipe involves going underneath a house and removing the entire old galvanized and cast iron pipe structure and replacing it with new copper tubing.

When Jeff and I opened the crawl space underneath the house, it looked like no one had been beneath this house for the entire 100 years. However, we were used to working in dirty environments, so we grabbed our tools and crawled underneath the house to begin what would be a four-day job. For three days, I connected new pipe making sure all of my welds with the torch were clean and precise. The work was difficult, and we always wore thick coveralls to protect ourselves as we crawled through dirt and over sharp rocks. Once engaged in the work it's not easy to take a coffee, food, or bathroom break. It's more productive to stay under for as long as possible and get as much done, because it was difficult getting in and out of a very tight crawl space, and time consuming to clean the dirt out of my hair, nose, shirt, underwear, pants, shoes, and socks!

On the fourth and final day, I stayed underneath the house from sun up till almost sun down with hardly a break. I wanted to finish this job and move on to something easier like repairing a leaky faucet or unplugging a garbage disposal.

When I finished connecting my last pipe, I called above for my father-in-law to turn on the water so I could test the new plumbing. He turned on the water full power, and with a light I checked every connection to make sure there were no leaks. With confidence and an inward joy, I announced that there were no leaks and everything looked fine. With the good report they hollered for me to come up and get ready to go. I carefully grabbed all my tools and began my long and final crawl through the dirt underneath the house toward the open crawl space.

Emerging, I took a deep breath of fresh air and thought how nice it was to see the beautiful Southern California sunset. I loaded all my tools into my plumbing van and shook out my dirty coveralls. Jeff and Bill commended me on a job well done, and we confirmed the next few days' assignments. Then they left in their work truck to check on a job on the other side of the county. I finished putting away my tools and was closing the van's cargo door when I realized something was missing—my pipe-cutting saw. Suddenly I realized exactly where I had left it—beneath the house in the farthest corner away from the crawl space entrance.

My heart sank, and I started to open my mouth to complain, but I caught myself just before the words escaped my lips. I said out loud, "No, I'm not going to complain. Lord, I wish I had not left my saw underneath the house, but since I have to go and get it, I'll just praise you as I go." I'll tell you right now, it wasn't easy for me to praise the Lord, but that's why the Bible speaks of the *sacrifice* of praise.

By him [Jesus] *therefore let us offer the* **sacrifice of praise** *to God continually, that is, the fruit of our lips giving thanks to his name* (Hebrews 13:15).

A sacrifice indicates that it is not always easy, that's why it's of great value when we praise God when things don't always go our way or when it's difficult. Anyone can praise the Lord when everything is going great; when there's plenty of money in the bank, when there's no pain in your body, and when everybody thinks you are great. But it takes a mature believer to rise up and praise the Lord when it appears everything's going backward instead of forward. True faith is not based on feelings, but on the Word of God.

As I pulled on those dirty coveralls and crawled back underneath the house with an electric powered light in my hand, I began to lift my praises to the Lord: "Lord I praise you! Jesus you are the best! Jesus you are Number One! Lord, even though I'm crawling through the dirt and rocks right now, I believe You have a high calling for me into the ministry, and I give You praise for it. I praise You. I praise You. I praise You!"

After a few minutes of crawling underneath the entire house I could see the saw lying in the dirt in the very back corner. When I finally was able to grab my saw, I made the turn for home and began to praise the Lord as I crawled on my belly while using my hands to help push through the dirt. By this time, I had been praising the Lord for about ten minutes, and I was beginning to sense the presence of the Lord. As I crawled along, singing and blessing the name of the Lord, my left hand suddenly struck something metallic. I swung my light over and saw a piece of metal just barely sticking up out of the ground. I dug down about two inches and to my surprise I pulled up the keys to my plumbing van!

"Dear Lord, these must have fallen out of my pocket today when I was working. You've helped me find them even before I knew I lost them!" Finding those keys was a real blessing because I didn't have a spare set. Finding them saved me from calling a locksmith and wasting several hours. One thing's for sure, I never would have found them on my own, the keys were not even visible beneath the dirt.

I believe that through this experience the Lord was trying to make a point to me. If I had not been praising the Lord, I am convinced I would have never found those keys. God is willing to help us; but we must be willing to praise Him on a continual basis.

PHYSICAL AND VERBAL BEATINGS

There is an interesting story found in the Book of Acts that demonstrates another example of what can happen when we praise the Lord at all times.

> *The crowd rose up together against them, and the chief magistrates tore their robes off them and proceeded to order them to be beaten with rods. When they had struck them with many blows, they threw them into prison, commanding the jailor to guard them securely, and he, having received such a command, threw them into the inner prison and fastened their feet in the stocks. But about midnight Paul and Silas were **praying and singing hymns of praise to God**, and the prisoners were listening to them; and suddenly there came a great earthquake, so that the foundations of the prison house were shaken; and immediately all the doors were opened and everyone's chains were unfastened (Acts 16:22-26 NASB).*

In this story, two godly and holy men encounter trouble and suffering for having done the right thing, which in this case was an act of Spirit-inspired boldness and power to deliver a young slave girl who was possessed with a spirit of divination. This difficult trial befell Paul and Silas as they were on their way to a prayer meeting.

Many Christians fail to understand that there are times when God will purposely allow us to walk through difficult experiences in life with His intention to develop in us the qualities that reflect the nature and character of our Lord. I'm not saying God does bad things to us, but I am saying that there is a road of the just and upright that we are required to walk that at times brings inescapable persecution. Although persecution is never enjoyable, it does have a positive inward effect causing us to humble ourselves and draw nearer to God to receive His strength. In situations of difficulty when God does not intervene, we must not seek deliverance, but rather the inward spiritual development that God is looking for in mature believers.

Paul and Silas were severely beaten with rods and then roughly thrown into jail without a trial. The act of beating someone with rods was not under the Jewish 40-stripe limitation associated with whipping a prisoner. The phrase, *"When they had struck them with many blows..."* implies they were hit so many times that they gave up counting.

I have discovered that although we may not suffer the physical beatings that Paul, Silas, and other Christians around the world endure, there is still a great amount of persecution here in the United States. Here we experience verbal abuse, and not so often physical. The tongue has great power to abuse. Lies, gossip, slander, and other forms of venomous attacks can often assail ministers and saints who are living right for God. One thing about being a minister in the United States is that you have to possess a heart like a lamb while having a tough exterior like an elephant. If you don't have a tough exterior then the cruel words that misinformed people speak can penetrate and create deep wounds that cause considerable pain.

After a brutal beating, the prisoners of this era in Roman history would then have a bucket of salt water poured on their backs to keep the maggots away from the wounds—this was the extent of prison hygiene and steps to prevent the spread of infection and disease. The jailer took extra caution to securing Paul and Silas in the inner most prison where it was cold, dark, damp, and dirty. Their feet were fastened securely in the stocks. I can't help but smile and think about how God delights in reclaiming what the devil used to inflict pain and suffering and turns it around as a means of deliverance for His children.

Now Paul and Silas joined good company with other men of the Bible who were also put in stocks—including Jeremiah and Joseph.

Jeremiah the prophet felt the backlash of the enemy for delivering the true prophetic Word.

> *Pashur had Jeremiah the prophet beaten and put him in the stocks that were at the upper Benjamin Gate, which was by the house of the LORD* (Jeremiah 20:2 NASB).

Joseph also suffered for having done the right thing, and found himself in a perplexing place that an all-wise and tender God chose in order to develop the leadership qualities within Joseph. These qualities would allow him to one day govern the most powerful nation on the face of the earth.

There in prison, they bruised his feet with fetters and placed his neck in an iron collar (Psalm 105:18 NLT).

In what is considered to be the oldest book in the Bible, we see Job crying out to God as he suffers great distress due to the calamities that have come against him. In his limited knowledge of spiritual matters, Job accuses the Lord of having trapped him. Job did not know that satan was the source of the evil that was taking place in his life.

You put my feet in the stocks And watch all my paths; You set a limit for the soles of my feet, While I am decaying like a rotten thing, Like a garment that is moth-eaten (Job 13:27-28 NASB).

Although Paul and Silas were having a very tough day, they looked to the Lord in the midnight hour. Many times it's at the darkest hour when God chooses to perform a miracle.

But about midnight Paul and Silas were praying and singing hymns of praise to God. Notice it says they were praying **and** singing hymns of praise to God. We should always pray, but there comes a time when the Lord wants to receive praise from our lips. For the most part, many of God's people are doing fine when it comes to praying, but praising often comes up short. We need to keep it balanced and make sure we are strong on giving God praise.

Paul and Silas were praising God out loud, *"...and the prisoners were listening to them."* Paul and Silas were not shy or embarrassed about what the other prisoners thought. It was after prayer **and praise** when things got very interesting!

"...and suddenly there came a great earthquake." I like it when God moves suddenly and shakes things up. I don't mind

waiting with faith and patience, but a sudden burst of God's power is something I'm always willing to accept.

"...and immediately all the doors were opened and everyone's chains were unfastened." God can use you to loose the chains of others, when you praise Him. God has the power to open every shut door and unloose every chain of bondage. As we praise Him continually we will see marvelous miracles.

LOST AND FOUND

Not long ago, my wife and I had just arrived back in Moravian Falls, North Carolina, after having been on the road for over a month preaching in other states. When we arrived, we stayed for a few days at a lodge situated on a mountain with beautiful views. I was informed that a large church group would soon be arriving at the lodge to stay for the weekend. I noticed that the owner of the lodge had asked her son, who was the same age as me, to spread some pine needles around the front of the lodge to make it look prettier because most of the grass was dead due to the cold, winter weather.

I looked out of my window and watched him working as he was taking large bales of pine needles and spreading them over the front lawn. As I watched him work I told the Lord, "I don't think he's going to get that done before the group shows up. Lord, I'll go give him a hand." I have discovered that people like it when a minister acts normal and doesn't pretend to be so holy.

I offered to help out, and he gladly accepted my proposal. I grabbed a big bundle of pine needles and began spreading. We both worked very fast and hard and unloaded an entire pickup truck full of pine needle bales and spread them evenly over a large area in only 20 minutes. When we finished working, we were soaking wet with sweat despite the 40-degree temperature.

As we stood there trying to catch our breath while enjoying the new look we had given to the front lawn, I couldn't help but notice a small little area of pine needles that did not look as smoothly laid as I wanted them to appear. As I walked out over the area of pine needles that we had just spread, I came to the small part that I wanted to touch up on. When I reached down to spread the pine needles more evenly, my hand touched something that made a metallic clink sound. I dug down through the 6-inch layer of pine needles, curious to see what caused the faint noise. To my surprise, I found the keys to my car! I checked my coat pocket and realized my keys were gone. They must have fallen out when I was working, and having been so caught up in my work I didn't even notice when they slipped out.

"Lord, you've helped me find them before I even knew I lost them—again!" The Lord is so good; He's always looking out for us. If later on I had noticed my keys were missing, I never could have found them under all of the pine needles—it would have been like trying to find a needle in a haystack, or should I say a pine-needle stack?

For some time the experience with the keys was a little puzzling to me. First of all, I am not the type of person who loses things, so having had that happen to me twice roused my spiritual curiosity. I didn't spend too much time thinking about it, but rather just continued walking closely to God and doing the work of the ministry.

About a month went by and my family and I were back out on the road again ministering. This time we were in Northern

Virginia where we were holding revival meetings at a local church for four days. On the last day of the meeting, my wife and daughter went into town to get some lunch while I stayed behind in the hotel room to continue praying for the evening service. As I was in the hotel room alone, I was slowly pacing back and forth while lifting my hands and praising the Lord. Suddenly, an angel came into the room and stood two feet behind my left shoulder. I stopped and stood completely still, as a glorious wave of peace and energy emanated from the angel and rushed throughout my entire body. This divine energy produced heavenly warmth inside of me which caused a deep sense of well-being to flood my soul.

The angelic messenger said, *"That's why you were allowed to find lost keys, because **praise is the lost key to victory**."* After he spoke, I began to reverently praise and worship the Lord knowing that I had just received a vital spiritual truth. Since that day, I have taken extra time each day to make sure I praise God more often. The Lord has blessed me so richly for taking the time to give Him praise.

After I received this particular angelic visitation, a few days went by and I was in an intimate time of prayer with God. While in this secret place of prayer, I asked the Lord why the angel said, *"...praise is the lost key to victory."* "Lord, why did the angel say that praise is a *lost key*?"

The Lord responded clearly to me, "It is a lost key because most of My people don't praise Me. At times they will praise Me when things go well, but when faced with difficulties and trials there is little or no praise." Now I believe I understand more clearly why Jesus cried out while on the Cross: *"I thirst!"* (John 19:28b).

Even though the Lord was suffering great physical thirst, I believe there is a deeper expression. Our Lord is thirsty for praise. So many of His people praise Him on Sunday, but on the other six days of the week they never give the Lord any water to drink! We have the ability to quench His thirst by taking extra time to praise Him each day of our lives.

I have discovered that praise is an expression of our faith in God that demonstrates to Him that we believe we have received that which we asked of Him in prayer.

> *Therefore I say to you, whatever things you ask when you pray, believe that you receive them, and you will have them* (Mark 11:24 NKJV).

Many Christians have caught the revelation of speaking words that express their faith in having received a promised blessing. Even before the miracle takes place where the object of desire is seeable or can be touched, many Christians have matured to a place where they can *"call those things that be not as though they were"* (Rom. 4:17). The proper understanding of *"I have it now before I ever see it"* is an essential requirement when it comes to receiving from God by faith.

However, the Lord wants us to come to an even higher level of relationship with Him where we not only speak words of faith, but put action behind our words as well. How do we express a higher level of faith that goes beyond the necessity of making positive statements with our lips? I believe this can be accomplished through what I call the declaration of "Dance in Advance." If a person really believes by faith they already have what it is they asked for in prayer, then there is cause for considerable celebration.

What better way to celebrate and thank God for answering your prayer than praising Him with singing and dancing? *Dance in advance* and praise God before you ever see your miracle. Dance your miracle all the way into your life by giving God the praise He deserves, and I'm not talking about what you do on Sunday while at church. I'm talking about Monday morning when you feel no anointing, and Tuesday evening when there appears to be no hope on the horizon. Dance and praise God on Thursday when nobody else can see you but God Himself.

Prove to God that you truly believe the miracle is done before you ever see it by praising him with all of your heart. As you praise God your miracle is moving closer and closer to you. God has heard your prayer, and He has already said, "Yes." There's no more need to keep bringing the request before God. Just praise Him now and thank Him that it's done. As you do, you will find yourself enjoying sudden and glorious breakthroughs, while having the time of your life as you run with the horses and walk with the angels!

REFLECTIONS ON PRAYER
AND FASTING

REFLECTIONS ON PRAYER
AND FASTING

Prayer and fasting can play an important role in your life when it comes to drawing nearer to God; but I want to share a few things on this subject from a different point of view. In 2003, my wife and I lived in Long Beach, California. We had lived there for almost three years when an interesting event took place.

One day, I had gone out to the garage to pray because it would be quiet, and I would not be distracted. As I knelt down and began to pray, I could still hear just a little bit of noise coming from inside the home, so I decided to sit inside Kelly's car which was parked in the garage. At that time Kelly had a purple PT Cruiser with a custom license plate: ROYAL PT. I got into the car, closed all the doors, and it was completely quiet which is just the way I like it when I pray.

After I had been praying for about 45 minutes, I began to strongly sense the presence of the Lord, so I lifted up my hands and began to worship God and bless His name. As I did, I suddenly heard a strong wind blow into the car with a loud "Swooosh" sound. As I heard that sound I felt the rear of the car go down several inches caused by increased weight.

With my eyes closed in worship, I said, "Lord, two angels just came in and sat in the back seat of the car, didn't they?" To my surprise, a male voice answered me and said, "Yes, they did." The voice seemed audible to my natural and spiritual ears, and seemed to be right next to me. It has been through times like this when I have learned to *lean in* on a vision from God and receive what He has to offer.

When you are having a vision you must be careful to not pull out of it by allowing your mental reasoning to interfere. During a vision is *not* the time to open your eyes, start looking around, trying to figure out what's taking place. Just *lean* in to a visitation when it comes to you.

Since I knew the Lord was near, I pushed a little deeper and said, "Lord, why are they here?" The Lord said, "They are here to help you during your times of prayer and fasting." I said, "Thank you, Lord. I receive the ministry of these two angels." I paused for a moment and then said, "Lord, what are their names?" The Lord said, "Joash, and Josiah." When the Lord said that, I slowly turned around and looked in the back seat of the car.

Sitting there I saw two angels with beautiful crimson red robes. The robes were stained with such a deep red color that where the folds of the robe were, the fabric looked almost black. Both angels were strikingly majestic, having shoulder-length hair that was as black as onyx, and eyes the color of black Tahitian pearls. They were staring right at me with a look that suggested they were ready to start their assignments.

As I looked at them, I began to slowly turn my attention forward, while reverently giving God thanks for sending the angels. Suddenly, as I turned toward the front, all the hair on the back of my neck stood completely up, as there sitting in the front seat of the car next to me was the Lord Jesus Christ. Seeing Him completely took my breath away, and I pushed myself as far against my door as possible as I looked at Him in awe. This was the first time I ever saw the Lord.

"Lord!" I said. He gently gave me a joyful smile as He seemed to have enjoyed catching me totally off guard. As I looked at Him I noticed He was wearing a *royal purple* robe that had a solid gold sash around His waist. The Lord also had a gold miter (a royal crown) around His head. He had gold sandals on His feet and He had what appeared to be light, sandy-brown hair that fell almost to His shoulders. As I looked at Him, He crossed His hands together in His lap and put His head down as He began to pray for the ministry He had for me to fulfill. I simply put my hands in the air and reverently began to worship God. The Scripture came to me from Hebrews of how He is always praying for us.

> *But He, because He continues forever, has an unchange-able priesthood. Therefore He is also able to save to the uttermost those who come to God through Him,* **since He always lives to make intercession for them** (Hebrews 7:24-25 NKJV).

The Lord has quite a sense of knowing how to connect things and people. He appeared to me while wearing a royal

purple robe as I sat in the purple ROYAL PT Cruiser. Everything about the Lord is first-class.

As the vision lifted, and I stepped out of the car, the first thing I did was grab my concordance which was lying on a shelf in the garage. I looked up the names Joash and Josiah to see what they meant in the original Hebrew language. *Joash* means "he who burns." *Josiah* means "the Lord burns." Prayer combined with fasting certainly produces an inward purging by the Spirit of God that burns away the desires of the flesh. Prayer combined with fasting helps burn up the desires of our carnal nature by keeping the self-life in a subdued and crucified position.

FASTING AND FEASTING

I remember the pastor at the church I attended in high school. He was a wonderful preacher, and he was the first minister who ever spoke to me about the Lord having a call for me into the ministry. He was very nice, and he was very overweight. This may sound a bit strange, but I have seen him and other ministers who teach about fasting who are overweight. This puzzled me for some time, until I realized what was taking place. Those ministers were truly fasting, but they overate *before* the fast and then would eat extra meals *after* the fast to make up for missed meals.

I have personally fasted frequently in the past when I would not eat for several days. One time, I even did a 40-day fast with no food and only water and apple juice to drink. I lost 22 pounds, which is a lot to lose when you only weigh 145 pounds. Today, I am always open to the Holy Spirit's leading to fast should He direct me to; but what I have learned over the years is that it is more spiritually productive and physically healthier to live a *fasted lifestyle*.

A fasted lifestyle is choosing to never eat all you want. When I notice that I'm getting close to being full I simply stop eating, even if it means I didn't clean my plate. Somebody may say, "You should eat everything on your plate because there are starving children in Africa!" Well, that guilt tactic doesn't work for me.

The first time I went to Africa to minister in a crusade I just about preached myself into the ground ministering three times a day for several weeks in services that sometimes lasted four hours. It was a tough ordeal, but God blessed the meetings and wonderful miracles took place.

About a year later, Kelly and I invited the host pastor to spend several weeks with us in California so he could be refreshed and see the United States. While staying with us in our home he confided in me that when he saw me for the first time at the airport a year earlier for the East African meetings he was greatly concerned that I would not be a good preacher. His perception was that only preachers from the United States with huge bellies could preach well. In his country in Africa they admire preachers who are overweight, so he was greatly concerned about my ability to minister. After hearing me preach, he said he was glad to know that it is possible to minister and do a great job without having a large belly.

Personally, I am in the ministry for the long haul. I don't plan on shutting things down prematurely because my body can't go any further due to sickness and disease. Some Christians want God to heal them from physical ailments when, in many cases, all they need to do is adopt a healthier diet and eat in moderation—most of their health-related problems would disappear. Living a fasted lifestyle is often difficult because the carnal nature wants to eat the whole pie, not just a slice. Prayer combined with a fasted lifestyle serves the purpose of denying the flesh its carnal desires and helps us to *die daily*, not just when we happen to be fasting.

Some Christians mistakenly think that their fasting will change God. But fasting does not change God—He is the same before we fast, while we fast, and He will be the same after we have fasted. Fasting changes us and helps subdue the carnal nature. If fasting did change God then I would fast until my teeth fell out, and I'm sure you would too. I talked with a minister over a year ago who told me he read of several instances when certain ministers who lived long ago had done so much fasting that their teeth did fall out!

A person should have enough common sense to realize that if God put teeth in our mouths, than we shouldn't do anything that causes us to lose them. God gave us food to enjoy; it is a blessing from the Lord. Chewing strengthens the gums which support the teeth. If a person doesn't chew or exercise his teeth for a long enough period of time then there will eventually be a need for dentures. Eating is a good thing, and we should enjoy our food, in moderation.

I am not by any means against fasting, but I believe it needs to be kept in its proper place. Nowhere in the New Testament is the Church commanded to follow any required methods or periods of fasting. It should simply be kept open to the Holy Spirit's leading. Also, fasting without time well spent in prayer will not affect much of an inward spiritual change. Fasting without prayer will lead to irritability, mood swings, and a lost opportunity for spiritual renewal.

Living a fasted lifestyle allows you to be sensitive to the Holy Spirit on a consistent basis. Usually, before I minister I will eat very light, or maybe not eat at all if I am not hungry at the time. If I feel a little weak, then I'll grab something small to hold me over until I've finished ministering for the day. The two angels the Lord gave me have helped train me to not overeat but to enjoy the blessing of a good meal. I pray that the Lord helps you, too, to find that delicate balance so you can fully enjoy a fasted lifestyle and live in divine health.

DIVINELY GRANTED
VISIONS AND DREAMS

DIVINELY GRANTED
VISIONS AND DREAMS

After spending time in prayer, I thought it would benefi-
cial to include some of the visions and dreams that the Lord
has granted me to experience. I pray these will be for your
spiritual enrichment and that you may glean nuggets of truth
that will strengthen you in your desire to draw nearer to God.
I also pray that as you read these experiences that the Holy
Spirit will bless you to receive a refreshing cascade of visions
and dreams that will sweep you away into the Presence of
our Lord.

THE DIAMOND OF HOPE

In the Church today many of us have been enlightened
through good Bible teaching on the subject of faith. The subject of Bible faith is a foundational topic that every Christian

should be well-skilled in. *Faith* can be described as "an absolute and complete trust in God and His Word." *Hope* can be defined as "an eager, joyful expectation that is produced by knowing that one's faith in God will produce a miracle." Faith and hope work together.

We see in the life of Abraham that he did not allow his hope for a promised son to slip away. God promised Abraham that he and Sarah would have a son. In the natural, this was an impossible situation because Abraham was nearly 100 years old and Sarah was an old woman who had been barren all her life. Paul spoke of Abraham's response to this situation in the book of Romans.

> Against all **hope**, Abraham in **hope** believed and became
> the father of many nations, just as it had been said to him,
> "So shall your offspring be" (Romans 4:18 NIV).

In order to interpret this verse correctly, it is necessary to understand that there are two kinds of hope mentioned in the Bible. First, there is a natural hope which anybody can have. Second, there is a divine hope which only God can impart into our hearts by the Holy Spirit. Let's first examine what natural hope is.

Natural hope is the kind of hope that can leave you very, very disappointed. Many people go to Las Vegas with a great hope that they are going to beat the odds and win the jackpot. Very few of these people ever win any kind of substantial money. Even when many have gambled all their money away, others still hope that their last roll of the dice will be the one that makes all the losing pay off. When dealing with natural hope, the odds are always stacked against you because you are operating on satan's turf, and he rules in the area of luck and chance.

God wants everyone to be blessed, not just someone chosen by a roll of the dice.

Natural hope is what was staring Abraham in the face. Natural hope can join up with doubt and unbelief to make situations appear hopeless. Have you ever experienced this feeling? I'm sure you can relate to how Abraham felt. Anyone who follows the Lord with his or her whole heart will eventually be led into a place that in the natural looks hopeless. This is a place where the Lord expects us to mature and walk by faith and not by sight. During such trying times we must joyfully expect our miracle, even when there is no hope in the natural.

It is important to realize that Abraham did not deny his present, physical condition or the bareness of Sarah's womb. He was aware of these conditions. But against *natural hope* he believed in *divine hope* that God would fulfill His promise. *Divine hope* that comes from God will never disappoint you. This kind of hope actually creates an inner confidence that is expressed through a joyful expectancy. You may not know how God is going to fulfill His Word to you, and you may not know when it is going to happen, but in your heart you know it's already a done deal. Hallelujah! Divine hope makes you want to praise the Lord. I believe in divine hope just like Abraham did.

HOPE AGAINST HOPE

I want to share with you a remarkable experience that occurred in my life that I believe will stir up God's hope within you. As mentioned previously, when Kelly and I lived in Long Beach, California, I would often go out to our garage and pray. The garage was attached to our house, so it was a convenient place to go for privacy. One day, as I was praying I went into a trance. A trance is a type of closed vision that is mentioned in the Bible.

There are three types of visions: *spiritual vision*, a *closed vision*, and an *open vision*. A *spiritual vision* is what you see with the inner eyes of your spirit. A spiritual vision can also be described as an inner vision. A spiritual vision is what is reflected upon the canvas of your imagination, which then forms as a thought within your mind. For this reason those who are called into the ministry as prophets have to be very careful about what they watch on television or movies because they depend upon having spiritual sight. It's important to not "muddy the waters" of one's imagination, but rather maintain a pure thought life.

A *closed vision* is when your physical senses are suspended, and you are not aware at the moment of your natural, physical surroundings. In a closed vision, you only see the spiritual world and none of the physical world. A closed vision usually takes place in a state of trance. This is what took place with Peter when he was on the rooftop and fell into a trance and had the vision of the large sheet descending from heaven containing various types of animals. (See Acts 10:9-16.)

An *open vision* is when you see into the spirit realm and the natural realm at the same time. An open vision occurs with your natural eyes open, thus opening the natural and spiritual realms simultaneously.

As I was in the garage praying, I fell into a trance and suddenly heard a loud suction-type sound. Before I knew it, I was being lifted up and pulled through white clouds at a fantastic rate of speed. As my velocity of travel began to slow down, I came to a stop as my feet touched down with a thud on a solid foundation.

As I began to look around, I saw the most beautiful colors of light. The two primary colors I saw were gold and orange which were often blended together as they moved through the air before me to form a sherbet-orange color—reminding me of the push up ice cream pops that I ate as a little boy. The colors were dazzling and brilliant, but soft and warm at the same time. The colors were going all through me, and I could sense energy and power carried by waves of radiant light.

As I stood there, I turned my attention to directly in front of me where I saw the largest throne I had ever seen. It must have been 70 feet tall and was completely covered in a glistening white cloud. All I could see were the two armrests of the throne extending outward from the cloud. I instantly knew I was standing before the Heavenly Father. I had never felt more comfortable in all my life as I did standing there.

As thoughts of overwhelming peace flooded the depths of my soul, I stood in amazement as two large hands emerged from the cloud toward me. I saw the robe of God that covered the Father's arms. The robe was gleaming white and thick and luxurious as it draped down to the wrist area of His hands. His hands were enormous, and with them He gently picked me up and pulled me inside of the cloud of glory that covered His throne. He set me on His lap and held me tight with His arms securely wrapped around me.

I grabbed the Father and plunged my face deep into His thick, lush robe. I could actually smell the fragrance of God, which is utterly pure, beyond description. The Father gave

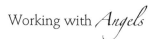

me a great big hug and then said to me, *"I love you."* Hearing that, I felt like I exploded into a million pieces on the inside. Every shortcoming in life was forgiven. All the times I had failed and let myself and others down was immediately wiped away. Every disappointment I ever went through in life was removed by those three words.

When this experience took place, I was in my late thirties and had never heard my natural father say to me, "I love you." Although I know he has always loved me, he came from an older generation that did not have the liberty and freedom to express those feelings with words. My heavenly Father completely filled every gap and void by speaking those words of blessing over me. My smile that day was bigger than the state of Texas.

After a few moments, the Father kissed me on the forehead, and then picked me up and gently placed me on my feet about 15 feet from His throne. As I looked again at the cloud of glory covering His throne, I knew something was about to be imparted to me. I bowed on my right knee, and as I did, the right hand of God came forth out of the cloud and stopped just in front of me. This time His hand was closed, and I knew the Father had a gift for me. As I watched, He slowly opened His hand, and there resting in His palm was an exquisite, stunning blue diamond necklace.

The necklace was comprised of a large center, blue marquis diamond with smaller blue diamonds making up the rest of the strand. As I knelt, He lovingly placed the necklace around my neck. Then I stood up and lifted the necklace up from my chest to take a closer look at it. The diamonds all appeared to be filled with some type of mysterious liquid blue fire. The colors were a deep, dark translucent blue that seemed to represent one of the attributes of God.

I said, "Father, what is this gift?" He replied, *"It is the Diamond of Hope."* He continued, *"Hope is a divine expectation that what I have promised you can come to pass at any moment."* The Father paused just a moment before slowly speaking to me, *"Your hope is well-pleasing to me."*

Deeply touched, I said, "Thank you Father, I receive this precious gift." As I lifted my hands to worship God and to bless His name I was completely surprised to find myself back in the garage on my knees. Upon recognizing I was back, it took a few minutes to adjust from coming out of such an experience. I could hardly walk, and it was difficult to breathe because of the weight of the Presence of the Lord that I continued to so strongly sense. There's something wonderful about the Lord's Presence that makes everything slow down in the natural.

After this vision was completed, I felt led by the Holy Spirit to meditate upon the statement that Peter made in his epistle to the women in the early Church.

> *Your beauty should not come from **outward** adornment, such as braided hair and the wearing of gold jewelry and fine clothes. **Instead, it should be that of your inner self,** the unfading beauty of a gentle and quiet spirit, which is of great worth in God's sight* (1 Peter 3:3-4 NIV).

God is more interested in our inward adornment than in our outward appearance. We should do our best to make a good outward presentation, but we should put the highest priority on adorning the inner man. In this present life, we do not see with our natural eyes the inner man. Our inner being is hidden from our natural eyes.

As we take hold of and walk in revelation truth from the Word of God, then we position ourselves to receive precious gifts of adornment that the Father may choose to grant to us.

After this vision, the Lord also reminded me of the time my parents took my two brothers and I to Washington, D.C., to visit the Smithsonian Museum of Natural History. I was probably only nine or ten years old, but I remember seeing something that particularly stood out to me, and we had to stand in a long line to view it. It was displayed in a safe that had a glass door, and two armed guards stood on either side of this particular exhibit. Of course I'm talking about the famous "Hope Diamond."

Kelly and I visited the same museum while in Washington last year, and I noticed the layout was different since I was there in the mid 1970s. The Hope Diamond is displayed as the premier attraction in the center of a room that contains some of the most well-known pieces of jewelry in the world. The Hope Diamond slowly revolves on a pedestal behind a shield of 3" bulletproof glass. It is the largest and most perfect blue diamond in existence. The diamond pendant is displayed in the setting of a necklace against a backdrop of soft blue velvet.

So many things we see in the natural can be traced back to their original source in the Spirit. I want to encourage you today to release your hope in God. He will not disappoint you. Allow divine expectancy to flow out of you today and rejoice in faith that the miracle you desire is yours.

HELL'S KITCHEN

The subject of holiness is not mentioned often in churches today. Unfortunately, the word *holiness* for many people conjures up thoughts of angry preachers throwing the Bible at their congregation for not being good enough. Other thoughts come to mind of old-time Pentecostal churches that do not allow the women to put on makeup or wear slacks. Some churches won't permit women to enter the church sanctuary if they are wearing slacks. Church leaders may think they have good reasons for these prohibitions, but many women just become frustrated and rebellious. Holiness is not a matter of rules, regulations, and dress codes. Those things do not make a person holy. However, Christians should want to dress modestly.

Once I had an unusually profound dream in which I was invited to a fabulous restaurant that served only the finest food at very expensive prices. The restaurant had a reputation for impeccable service and mouth-watering dishes. As I approached the restaurant, I noticed the stately Italian brick exterior and saw all the servers dressed in elegant-looking tuxedos. As I entered the restaurant, I was warmly greeted by the Maitre de' and was escorted to my table. While slowly walking to my table, the host tried to make me feel welcome by making an extremely derogatory comment about a well-known minister! He did not know that this was an insult to me. I immediately responded by saying how much I admired the television minister and that I was a financial supporter of his ministry. Completely caught off guard, the host quickly extended his hand to shake mine and offered an apology, not wanting to offend me or cause me to leave the restaurant. I accepted his apology and was then seated at my table.

While sitting at my table, I began to notice what others around me were eating. When I saw the food on their plates, I was immediately repulsed by the sight. It was the most despicable form of food I've ever seen. The people were eating what appeared to be demonic insects that were hideous beyond what words could describe. The Lord then spoke to me and said, *"This food comes from Hell's Kitchen. It's what the devil serves up for his people to eat all the time. It saddens me that many of My people are eating the same filth."*

Immediately, I looked around for the nearest exit, but I heard the Lord speak to me again. He said, *"Come, and I will show you where this food comes from."* I was taken to the back of the restaurant where the manager had assembled a small team of about ten workers to go with him and get the fresh catch of the day. Each worker put on what appeared to be a yellow, toxic-waste suit, the kind that allows you to work around dangerous radioactive waste. Each worker zipped up his or her suit that was enclosed from head to toe and walked out into what appeared to be a large, wildly-overgrown jungle. Every tree and plant in this demonic jungle was loaded with millions of spider webs, and the entire place was crawling with all forms of unclean creatures. In the dream, I was allowed to stand off at a distance and view this wickedly twisted sight.

It was difficult for me to watch because being so near to the jungle was extremely dangerous. Everything was highly toxic. I had to constantly shift my feet because the vines were spewing out acid as they moved on the ground like snakes and burned anyone or anything they touched. I saw insects that were so dangerous that if touched, they could instantly kill you.

A horrific spirit of fear saturated the entire dismal atmosphere of the jungle. I watched as the restaurant workers used special tools that were about 10 feet long which allowed them to reach up into tree limbs and grab vile-looking bugs, spiders, insects, ants, and other things too perverse to describe. Then they bagged these creatures and quickly took them back to the restaurant and eagerly served them to the people.

When I woke up from this dream, I knew the Lord was deeply grieved over many of His own people who regularly feast on the devil's food. In my heart, I saw a vision of a Christian man sitting in the comfort of his living room on Saturday night as he watched a murder mystery on television. The show pictured blood being shed, the glorification of immorality, and God's name being taken in vain. This show was a great insult to the Holy Spirit, yet the man disregarded the Spirit's leading to not watch the program. Such people are deceived in their own hearts because they think they can consume this type of entertainment, and it will have no negative affect on them. God is not mocked; He knows who is truly pure in heart.

HOLINESS IS STILL RIGHT

About a year ago, I awoke at 3 o'clock in the morning because I sensed the Lord wanted to speak to me. I quietly left the bedroom and went to an empty guest room in the house so I wouldn't disturb Kelly. I lay down on the guest bed for a few minutes and closed my eyes to rest a while. When I opened my eyes there were five angels standing around the bed in a semicircle. They were all smiling at me with big, beautiful smiles. One of the angels stepped forward and said, "We are the five angels of revival. We have come to teach you about the Spirit of Holiness."

These five angels had been involved in previous or ongoing revivals in different parts of the world. Out of the five angels, I only recognized one of them. This one particular angel appeared to look about 85 percent like the man whom he ministered along side of during a recent well-known revival

in the United States. Our ministering angels can sometimes take on similarities of our appearance. We see an example of this in the Book of Acts after Peter miraculously escaped from jail and went to a late night prayer meeting to inform the church of his escape.

> *Peter knocked at the outer entrance, and a servant girl named Rhoda came to answer the door. When she recognized Peter's voice, she was so overjoyed she ran back without opening it and exclaimed, "Peter is at the door!" "You're out of your mind," they told her. When she kept insisting that it was so, they said,* **"It must be his angel."** *But Peter kept on knocking, and when they opened the door and saw him, they were astonished* (Acts 12:13-16 NIV).

It seems the early church understood that one's personal angel can have similar appearance traits in relation to the individual they are assigned to. I believe this is why they said, *"It must be his angel."*

These five angels sat next to me on the bed and talked with me for 30 minutes about the importance of living a holy life. One of the angels stood out to me because of the tremendous humility that he carried. It was so captivating that I wanted to talk to him. I asked this angel, "What was it like to have been involved in the move of God that you experienced?" He replied, "Well, honestly, we didn't have too much to do with it. We simply went with the flow and God carried the whole thing."

I noticed that every time this angel spoke he always did so in a way that directed all the glory to God and not to men or angels. I could tell that the man whom this angel assisted in earthly ministry must have been a truly humble servant of God.

Before the angels left, they all looked at me with their radiant smiles which were so warming to my heart. The angel nearest to me said, "Would you like to experience what it is like to be in the center of a Heaven-sent, old-fashioned, full-blown move of God?"

"Yes!" I said.

(Just a little note as you are reading this story: when you are in a place where the Spirit of God is ministering to you, it is not the time to go to the bathroom or say, "I'm a little tired right now, can't we do this later?" Grab your blessing while you've got it in front of you, a second opportunity may not come around again for quite some time.)

When I said, "Yes!" all five of the angels reached out their hands, and they each gently touched me with just the tip of their pointer finger. Such power went into me that I immediately fell on the ground and shook intensely for two hours. The shaking was so strong that I remember being concerned about waking up Kelly from her sleep in the other room. Now I understand how the Quakers and the Shakers got their names! When God does a shaking in a person, He does it to shake out the chaff so that only the finest wheat remains.

Today, the Lord Jesus is preparing His Bride to soon come and be with Him. The Bride of Christ is without stain, or wrinkle, or any other blemish. May we prepare ourselves for the Lord's return by perfecting holiness in the reverence of the Lord.

THE FILTHY MAN

Many times when the Lord speaks to me through a dream it occurs just before I wake up in the morning. With one particular

dream, it ended as soon as I woke up and was so fresh on my mind that I could totally recall every detail with great clarity, from start to finish. However, this one dream that the Lord gave me was very unsettling. As a matter of fact, it was so upsetting to me that as soon as I sat up in bed, I told the Lord that I did not care if the dream was from Him or not. I told Him I didn't want to know the interpretation because the dream was so revolting that it brought a great disturbance when the images of the dream flashed through my mind.

Often I will tell my wife when the Lord speaks to me through a dream, but this time I didn't say anything. I simply wanted to dismiss the entire incident because it was so disturbing to me. Sometime later the Lord released me to share this dream with my wife and others. Please follow along with me as I share this dream with you.

I found myself walking through a great valley that appeared to be a sort of Valley of Death. There was a great multitude of people in this valley with me, and we were all moving forward without any hope. The line of people stretched as far back as I could see, and I was jammed in at the front along with thousands of others. The surrounding landscape was dark, dismal, and dreary. A thick, grey cloud hung over all the people; there was no laughter or joy, only a heavy weight of hopelessness.

Suddenly, I was removed from the crowd and found myself standing on a high plateau overlooking the dark valley and the massive river of suffering humanity. I could hear those at the front of the line talking. They were saying that something had to be done to absolve the problem of suffering. The line of people continued to move up a high hill where they stopped at a steep ledge on the top of the hill. There was a huge boulder there, and I heard them say if they could just throw that boulder off the cliff then their problems would be over. With great effort and exertion they pushed until the boulder toppled and fell over the ledge of the steep cliff and dropped with great force into what looked like a large lake of raw sewage.

The great impact created large splashing waves of green filth as putrid waters sprayed forth in all directions. Then to my shock and disgust, there came from up out of this lake where the boulder fell, a man covered from head to toe in raw sewage. He was lifted upward by the force of the boulder's impact, and everyone in the valley and those on the high hill could easily see him. It was the most horrific sight I have ever seen. The man was covered with sewage and had strands of filth hanging off of his body. The man's body was lifted upward, and his arms were outstretched. His feet were together. The stench and the filth were so repulsive that I turned my face away from the sight of the suffering man. At that point the dream ended, and I awoke and sat up in bed.

That whole day, I deliberately shut the dream out of my thoughts because it was upsetting to me. Late that evening, I took time to spend with the Lord in prayer. After praying for several hours I felt led by the Holy Spirit to take out my Bible and study a verse from Second Corinthians. This is the verse I was meditating on.

> *For you know the grace of our Lord Jesus Christ, that though He was rich, yet for your sakes He became poor, that you through His poverty might become rich* (2 Corinthians 8:9 NKJV).

The eighth chapter of Second Corinthians speaks about giving offerings. When verse nine is read in context with the entire chapter, it can be paraphrased as follows: For you know the grace (of giving) of our Lord Jesus the Anointed One, that though He was rich, yet for your sakes He became poor (upon the cross), that you through His poverty might become rich.

As I meditated on this verse and prayed in the Spirit, time went by, and it grew late into the night. I was walking around with my hands in the air and thanking and praising Him for redeeming me from the curse of poverty. While doing this I unexpectedly heard a calm, peaceful voice whisper to me and say, "That was Me." I recognized the voice as being the voice of the Lord.

I said to the Lord, "What do you mean by that?" Again he whispered, "That was Me."

At once the Spirit of the Lord quickened my understanding, and I shouted out, "I see it, Lord, I see it!"

This time when the Lord spoke to me, I could tell He was smiling because I had caught the revelation He was conveying to me. He said, "That's right, that was Me you saw in the dream. You saw Me not only bearing your sin, and the curse of the Law, you saw Me bearing your poverty as well. There is nothing holy about poverty. It is pure filth and a product of the curse. I took your poverty upon Myself and became poor for you so that you do not have to suffer poverty or lack, ever." He then added, "I did this on the Cross so that you might be rich."

The teaching that God wants His people to walk in financial freedom was not a new revelation to me. But, I was still left speechless from having gained a much stronger understanding of what the Lord endured on the Cross so that we may have the opportunity to experience redemption from the bondage of the spirit of poverty and lack. The Lord's grace of giving is marvelous toward us and has the potential to greatly affect our finances for the enrichment of our lives that we may be a blessing to others.

> *The blessing of the LORD brings wealth, and he adds no trouble to it* (Proverbs 10:22 NIV).

> *For he hath made him to be sin for us, who knew no sin; that we might be made the righteousness of God in him* (2 Corinthians 5:21).

> *All we like sheep have gone astray; we have turned every one to his own way, and the LORD has laid on him the iniquity of us all* (Isaiah 53:6).

THE YOUNG PROPHET

On the morning of May 15, 2002, I had a dream of great intensity in which the Lord spoke to me regarding a great shift in ministry that is coming. The dream had such an impact on me that for the first hour following the dream, it was difficult to function normally. I had to slow down as I did my necessary work and contemplate on what had just occurred. The carry over from the glory of God I experienced in this dream lasted throughout the day, making it almost impossible for me to not cry tears of love over anything that reminded me of the Lord. Here is the dream as the Lord shared it with me.

In the Spirit, I found myself traveling from church service to church service to see and listen in on some of the most well-known preachers in the world at that time. The services were held in church buildings, and some were held in large auditoriums. I was taken to many services and heard great

preaching from well-known and respected ministers. Many of these ministers are seen often on Christian television programs, and their faces are instantly recognizable. As I sat in these meetings, the Lord allowed me to watch each service and observe the minister who was preaching.

In each service, a measure of the Presence of the Lord could be sensed, The preaching was very good, but there were no miracles taking place, just good preaching. All of the ministers were dressed immaculately. Everything looked great, and the people in the services seemed to be having a good time. As I went from service to service, I noticed that each minister was very polished and delivered the message with eloquence in a style fitting his or her particular gifting. These were all Spirit-filled ministers, and each one could really preach, but I noticed no miracles were taking place. In some of the services, there were miracles, but nothing substantial that caused any kind of a stir.

Those present in the meetings would clap often and show their support of the message being preached. The people were happy and truly loved the Lord, but I strongly sensed that the people thought these types of services were the pinnacle experience of the Christian faith. They had no understanding that there was more God wanted to do, a lot more in fact.

Each time as I was taken to the next meeting there would be a slight pause of several seconds before the preaching started, and then I would watch the meeting begin. I viewed many meetings before I was taken to the final meeting. As usual, I experienced that slight pause of two or three seconds before the service started. During this tiny moment, I quickly noticed who the next preacher was!

Standing in the corner of a crowded meeting room was the preacher for the next service. He was wearing a faded white T-shirt and light-tan colored shorts that came down about two inches below his knee. His hair was golden brown, and it reached to his shoulders in length. To top it all off regarding his unusual attire, he had on construction boots, and the laces were not even tied! He had on white socks that came half way up his calves, and he appeared to be in his early thirties. I said out loud, "Who is this guy?" Then the service began, and I was in for a shock.

Without preaching or even greeting those who were in the service, he immediately walked out into the large group of people and called out a person on the right side of the room. At once, there was a noticeable change in the atmosphere as the glory of God came in and filled the room. The young minister began to give the Word of the Lord to this person, and the word spoken was so deep, so personal and intimate, that the person who received the prophetic word fell over and began sobbing uncontrollably.

The young minister then walked to another person and delivered another prophetic word that was so deep and accurate that the reverence of the Lord came strongly upon everyone present in the meeting. The individual who received the prophetic word also fell over and began to greatly weep, much like the first person. Suddenly, people all over the large room began repenting of hidden sins and making their hearts right with God.

The young prophet kept walking among the people speaking the Word of the Lord as the Holy Spirit led him. Every time a word was spoken, the individual would collapse in a heap of tears. The glory of God was so thick that it seemed as if you could take a knife and cut a chunk of it from the air. It was a weighty presence, affecting everybody in the meeting in a tangible way.

What was a blessing to me was that in the previous meetings I had witnessed I was allowed to view the meetings in the Spirit, but I was not involved in the meetings. However, in this meeting I was there as a participant and much to my delight the young prophet was now walking toward me!

As he drew nearer, I again noticed his untied construction boots and the simple clothing that he wore. There certainly wasn't anything glamorous about his clothing that would attract any attention to him. As he approached me, he smiled, thus making me feel comfortable and a little more relaxed. He stood in front of me and said, "You have a strong anointing." When he spoke those words to me, the glory of God intensified all around me, and I knew he was going to speak a word of instruction.

"Do you remember ten years ago how you used to train when you were involved in a certain athletic competition?" Within my heart, I knew exactly what he was referring to. Ten years earlier, I had been involved in a particular athletic event that consumed my time, money, and thoughts. The desire to succeed in this certain arena caused me to structure my life in a way that made everything else revolve around giving top priority to this activity. It was not uncommon for me to train four to six hours a day in this chief interest of mine, while being happy as a lark doing it. Not only did I physically train hard, but I studied the sport and read every book I could find on the subject to increase my knowledge. The sport consumed me.

Of course, I gladly forsook all of this when I was filled with the Holy Spirit and lost my appetite for worldly desires. In fact, it was several months after having been initially filled with the Holy Spirit when I took all of my trophies, medals, and other honors and tossed them in the trash dumpster behind the house I was staying in.

I nodded yes to the young prophet. I knew exactly what he was referring to when he mentioned the athletic competition from ten years earlier. Then he said, "You will have to be just as committed in this other area." In my heart I knew the other area he was referring to was the prophetic ministry. He looked at me and smiled, and as he did I felt all strength leave my body as I collapsed on the floor, weeping, because of the Lord's overwhelming presence.

As I awoke from this dream and talked to the Lord about what had taken place, the Lord impressed upon my heart several things. As I saw in the dream, the Lord has blessed the Body of Christ with fivefold ministry gifts whose ministries have been a blessing to all of us. The Lord will continue to work through these servants of His, but there is coming a great shift in ministry that will soon take place. When this occurs, the emphasis will not be on neatly packaged evangelical sermons or polished preaching, but rather on more of a display of the Word and the supernatural miracle-working power of God.

I'm all for good preaching, but when a preacher just walks off after a "good sermon" and never prays for people or steps out in faith to stir up the gifts of the Spirit, then it is an imbalanced presentation of the gospel. A great change is coming in this area.

My wife, who is very prophetic, sensed the Lord was speaking through the untied shoe laces of the prophet's boots. God does not want us tied up with the cares of this world. He wants us to be free (untied) to do the work (hence the construction boots) that He has prepared for us.

Today, the Lord is searching for those who are committed to pursuing Him above all other things. He desires to release end-time mantles and place a special anointing upon those who truly esteem Him as Lord. He is looking for yielded vessels through whom He may flow in great power without being hindered. May we all be diligent to allow Him to work in and through us.

> No one engaged in warfare entangles himself with the affairs of this life, that he may please him who enlisted him as a soldier (2 Timothy 2:4 NKJV).

> My message and my preaching were not with wise and persuasive words, but with a demonstration of the Spirit's power, so that your faith might not rest on men's wisdom, but on God's power (1 Corinthians 2:4-5 NIV).

ALL BARK AND NO BITE

Friends, who know me well, know that one of my favorite things to do is read. I love going to a bookstore and browsing through good books that interest me. Kelly actually has to give me a time limit on how long I can stay, or else I lose all track of time and would end up there all day.

Some time ago, I had completed all of the work scheduled for my day, and was looking for a little, recreational break. I spoke with Kelly and got the thumbs up to spend two hours at the bookstore. Going to the bookstore is a rare treat for me, and as I got out of the car and started to walk across the parking lot, my mind was already thinking of all the fun I was going to have catching up on some interesting books.

While crossing the parking lot, I had to walk around a row of vehicles parked closely together. The sun had gone down. It was dark outside, but there were overhead lights illuminating my way. When walking past a large, sport utility vehicle, I was suddenly startled by an explosive barrage of loud barking and vicious snarls coming from inside the vehicle, only inches away from my head! It was the most violent barking and snarling that I ever heard in my life.

I immediately jumped back with every hair on my head feeling like it was standing up. Adrenaline was surging through my body as I looked into the vehicle to see what had happened. It was dark outside, and all of the windows on this vehicle were heavily tinted. I noticed the back window had been left down about 10 inches, and it was through that window that I could see an enormous dog with a huge black head and red piercing eyes staring in anger right at me. This dog was so wild looking it must have belonged to the devil himself. Its tremendous bark had been so loud and unexpected that it left me quite startled, to say the least.

When having moved away to a safe distance, I looked at the dog and firmly said, "You have no authority over me." I didn't fully realize why I made this statement, but it just came up out of my spirit. I turned around and continued my walk across the parking lot toward the bookstore, but my nerves were still rattled from the dog's bark.

My joy of reading was gone, and I felt emotionally spent. As I kept walking forward, I was about ten feet from the entrance doors to the bookstore when I heard the voice of the Lord speak to me. The voice was audible to my spiritual *and* natural ears. The Lord said, "That's just like the devil, he's all bark and no bite!" At this point I stepped over to the side, away from the store entrance doors for a little privacy.

Then I poured out my heart to God, saying, "But Lord, that bothered me and was very upsetting."

He responded by saying, "Yes, I understand. But, you have not been harmed in any way. All the dog could do was bark and try to make you think it could hurt you, but it was actually limited in its ability to do so. Don't pay any attention to it, go on in the bookstore and have a good time. You'll be just fine, you'll see."

Do you know what? I took the Lord's advice and went into the bookstore and ordered a nice vanilla latte. Then I grabbed a bunch of good books and within ten minutes I was totally back to normal. Praise the Lord!

The devil really is defeated even if it does not appear to be so in the natural realm. My purpose for sharing this with you is to persuade you to not pay any attention to how the devil may be barking at you. The enemy can bark very loudly through negative circumstances in your life, such as children who have turned away from God, financial difficulties, health-related issues, and other seemingly hopeless situations. Even though you may be facing serious and legitimate problems, if you continue to believe God's Word over what the devil is trying to speak to you, you will eventually come through every storm in your life.

And having spoiled principalities and powers, he made a show of them openly, triumphing over them in it (Colossians 2:15).

Jesus triumphed over all the powers of darkness by His act upon the Cross. The forces of darkness have now been stripped and reduced to nothing when it comes to their ability to harm those who understand their authority in Christ. Jesus made a public spectacle of these defeated foes for all to see. Heaven, earth, and hell are aware that Jesus has been given all authority.

The imagery that Paul is portraying is clearly one that any Roman citizen of his era would understand. The terms used in this verse are all military. The term *spoil* refers to how the great Roman army would plunder the camps of their conquered enemies. During Paul's time, Rome was the world superpower and had the largest, most well-trained, and best-funded army in the world. When the Roman army overtook an enemy nation in battle, they would immediately put all the prisoners of war into chains and strip them of all their clothes to degrade and humiliate them. Then they would march them naked back to Rome that they might be displayed as conquered foes in a triumphal procession.

During these processions, the Roman citizens would mock, spit on, and hurl objects at the defeated army. The prisoners were made public spectacles before all of Rome as they were then led to the coliseum where the prisoners were executed. Having been an eyewitness to such spectacles, Paul fittingly describes the Lord's complete and total victory over the devil and all the powers of darkness.

It is important that we live closely to God so the devil finds no grounds of sin within us that would grant him legal access to do us harm. Sin is a door that gives the devil permission to gain access into our lives. What would have happened to me when I saw that dog in the vehicle if I had stuck my hand through the window and tried to pat him on the head? We all know the answer to that. He would have taken a big bite! When a person has pet, sin habits that are being cherished and held onto, they provide the devil with a big open window through which he will take a big inflicting bite. The results of such an attack are never pleasant, and always destructive.

> *He who digs a pit will fall into it, And whoever breaks through a wall will be bitten by a serpent* (Ecclesiastes 10:8 NKJV).

Breaking through God's wall of protection through acts of sin allows the devil to bite and inflict his venom which produces pain and suffering. While none of us are prefect, we can come into a place where we mature in our walk with God and walk under the wings of His protection.

Just recently, my wife and I were out on an extended ministry trip when we stopped during our travels to get a few things at a store in a small country town. We pulled our motor home into the parking lot, and my wife got ready to go into the store while I took our dog out for a little walk. It was a busy time of the day, and there were many people going to the store to buy groceries. I was walking our dog, Tabitha, who is a real sweet Airedale Terrier.

We had just begun our walk when we were approaching a stop sign. I couldn't help but notice a big, black pickup truck that was driving real slow as it pulled up to the stop sign on the opposite side of the street. As I watched, there before me unfolded an amazing scene that appeared to take place in slow motion. When the pickup truck came to a full stop at the stop sign, a huge head rose up from the back of the pickup truck. It was an enormous Rottweiler dog with dark, black-and-orange hair. When he saw me and my dog he became completely enraged. He placed his front paws up on the side of the truck and pushed off with all of his strength as he made a mad lunge toward me and my dog in a vicious attempt to attack us!

As he leaped in the air toward us, I heard a sudden *"Snap,"* as his leash got entangled on a hook within the bed of the pickup truck. The dog's forward progress was immediately stopped, and he was then roughly jerked back by the contraction of the leash, causing him to slam into the side of the pickup truck with a loud *"Thud."* He was left hanging there for about three seconds, suspended between heaven and earth, while he made gurgling sounds caused by the self-inflicted hanging.

The lady driving the truck jumped out and hollered with a thick southern accent, "You crazy dog!" She untangled him and struggled to lift him back up into the truck bed. She tied him securely and then quickly drove out of the parking lot. She never even said a word to me. It pays to be close to God and abide under the shelter of His wings! God will protect you from evil when you walk upright with Him.

So, if the devil has been barking at you lately, just keep on following Jesus and pay the enemy no attention. Spend extra time in the Word and prayer, and keep moving forward in faith. The goal of the enemy is to bluff you out of your faith with loud barking situations; but his barks are just a bunch of hot air. Yes, you may have a problematic situation. Do the

things in the natural that are in your ability to do, and trust God to do that which you cannot do. As you walk on in faith the empty threats of the enemy will trail off behind you, and you will see the reward of an enjoyable life that comes from trusting God.

Allow yourself the pleasure of racing with the horses, working with the angels, and walking closely with your heavenly Father.

Ministry Information

For information about the ministry of
STEVEN BROOKS INTERNATIONAL,
Please visit our Website at:
www.stevenbrooks.org

Additional copies of this book and other book titles from DESTINY IMAGE are available at your local bookstore.

Call toll-free: 1-800-722-6774.

Send a request for a catalog to:

Destiny Image® Publishers, Inc.

P.O. Box 310
Shippensburg, PA 17257-0310

*"Speaking to the Purposes of God for this
Generation and for the Generations to Come"*

**For a complete list of our titles,
visit us at www.destinyimage.com**